TEMPLES
IN THE
LAST DAYS

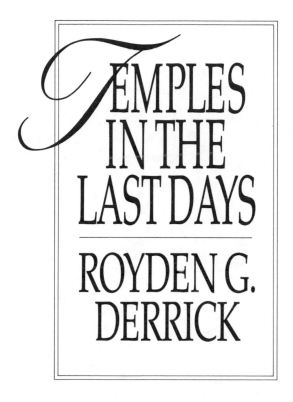

TEMPLES IN THE LAST DAYS

ROYDEN G. DERRICK

Bookcraft
Salt Lake City, Utah

Library of Congress Catalog Card Number: 87-72363
ISBN 0-88494-643-6

4th Printing, 1988

Printed in the United States of America

To Allie

Contents

◆

Preface

◆

The doctrine of The Church of Jesus Christ of Latter-day Saints is centered around Jesus Christ as the Savior of mankind. To members of the Church, temples are special places where worthy members make covenants with the Lord relating to principles of righteous living and receive sacred temple ordinances that relate to their eternal destiny. Having made these covenants and received these ordinances for themselves, they return to extend the temple blessings vicariously to their progenitors who had no such opportunity during their lifetime. In doing so, this selfless service builds in the participants spirituality and moral strength that prepares them for celestial glory. Thus the temple becomes a stepping stone to exaltation for those who participate and remain faithful. This practice, along with the supporting doctrine, came from God through his holy prophets and has been instituted in this dispensation of the fulness of times in preparation for the Lord's second coming.

In our premortal state we were spirits—spirit children of our Father in Heaven. When we were born into this world, our spirits were clothed with physical bodies of flesh and bones. God's plan of salvation was designed to enable us to regain his presence clothed with a refined and resurrected body. This mortal life is a probationary period wherein we prove ourselves by our willingness to accept Christ as our Redeemer and keep the commandments he has given us. These commandments have been given to us by his own voice and by the voice of his prophets through the ages, both ancient and modern, as documented in the scriptures.

At death our bodies go to the grave and our spirits go to the world of spirits. This is a place of preparation for resurrection, when our spirits will be reunited with our bodies. As we pass through the veil of death into the spirit world, we retain the intelligence we have gained in this life. We also retain our individual agency to think and act for ourselves.

Jesus Christ suffered in Gethsemane and gave his life on Calvary to atone for the sins of mankind. By this act of mercy, he satisfied the demands of eternal justice that a price be paid for the sins of those who are willing to follow him and who strive earnestly to keep his commandments. His having done so assures all mankind that their bodies will be reunited with their spirits at the time of resurrection; thus, he is our Savior. As we are resurrected, we also receive immortality, which is to live forever with the body and the spirit reunited. Immortality is a free gift from the Savior to each of us which requires no effort on our part.

The word *salvation* is used by various denominations to define eternal expectations. An understanding of life after death is uncertain in other Christian religions. Some people believe that salvation is to live with God with little or no understanding of what that entails. To the Latter-day Saint salvation is exaltation in the celestial kingdom of God. In the eternal future there will be three kingdoms, the highest of which is the celestial kingdom. Baptism is the gateway to the celestial kingdom.

The receipt of one's temple blessings—i.e., temple covenants and ordinances—is the gateway to exaltation in the celestial kingdom of God, which is the highest of three heavens or degrees within that kingdom. Here one will share the glory of the Father and live in his presence. All gospel ordinances must be ratified by the Holy Spirit of Promise, which is the Holy Ghost. This ratification is earned by striving to improve our lives and living in accordance with the commandments of God.

There are those who did not have the opportunity of hearing the gospel of Jesus Christ in mortality. To them the message is being taught by missionaries in the spirit world. Jesus himself organized this missionary force between the time of his crucifixion and his resurrection. Those who accept the gospel in the spirit world will need to receive the ordinance of baptism and other higher ordinances and make covenants with the Lord as the living do in the temple. Since these are earthly ordinances, they must be administered vicariously here in mortality for those who reside in the spirit world. To do this, each individual for whom the work is to be done must be uniquely identified. This is the reason why the Church and its members are so deeply engrossed in genealogical research. This process of family research and receiving vicarious ordinances for those who are unable to receive them for themselves develops a unity of love and respect not only for a person's immediate family but also for his ancestral family members and his posterity into the eternities. Since we are all from the family of Adam, this process unites the children of God and explains the statement of the Apostle Paul "that they without us should not be made perfect." (Hebrews 11:40.)

Prior to the time of Christ temples were used for performing sacred ordinances for the living and for sacrificial rites. Following the atonement of the Savior and his visit to the spirit world, where he organized missionary work, vicarious temple ordinances for the dead began. This is evidenced by the words of the Apostle Paul to the Corinthian Saints, "Else what shall they do which are baptized for the dead, if the dead rise not at all? why are they then baptized for the dead?" (1 Corinthians 15:29.) With the restoration of the gospel of Jesus Christ and the Church of Jesus Christ in these last days these sacred temple rites and ordinances for the living and the dead were restored. It is for this purpose that temples of The Church of Jesus Christ of Latter-day Saints pictured in this book are operating in various nations of the world.

Acknowledgments

◆

I humbly express gratitude to my Father in Heaven for promptings of the Holy Spirit which have given me a clearer understanding of the principles expressed in this book. When we ask him, he is a generous giver.

I express thanks to Audrey Jones, who encouraged me to write this series of articles and have them published so they could be widely shared. I express a special appreciation to Roy Doxey, who reviewed the manuscript and made helpful suggestions; to Dr. Thomas B. Smart, whose listening ear and analytical mind were helpful in furnishing direction and scriptural accuracy to the text; and to Ardyth Olen, who was supportive in typing the script and was patient with me in making changes.

I give special thanks to my devoted companion, Allie, who has been a continual inspiration to me and has contributed many helpful suggestions to these writings.

Finally, I give humble thanks and veneration to our Lord and Savior Jesus Christ, without whose teachings and atoning sacrifice we would have no hope of immortality, no opportunity of eternal life, no holy temples of the Lord, and hence no purpose for this book.

This is not an official Church publication, nor has its writing been prompted by any General Authority other than myself. I alone am responsible for the opinions and views it expresses.

KIRTLAND TEMPLE

And from this place they may bear exceedingly great and glorious tidings, in truth, unto the end of the earth, that they may know that this is thy work, and that thou hast put forth thy hand, to fulfill that which thou hast spoken by the mouths of the prophets, concerning the last days.

◆

From the dedicatory prayer by Joseph Smith
March 27, 1836

1
Temples of Former Dispensations

◆

Historically, a temple has been defined as a place set apart for sacred purposes. In a more restricted sense, a temple is a building constructed for and devoted to sacred rites and ceremonies. (See James E. Talmage, *The House of the Lord*, p. 1.) The Lord said, "My people are always commanded to build [a temple] unto my holy name" and further explained that it was for specific sacred purposes and "for the glory, honor, and endowment" of the Saints. (D&C 124:39.) Whenever circumstances have permitted, these temples have been elaborate buildings—for nothing is too good for the Lord. Elder Bruce R. McConkie said, "In the days of poverty, or when the number of true believers has been small, the Lord has used mountains, groves, and wilderness locations for temple purposes." (*Mormon Doctrine*, p. 780.)

A temple is characterized not only as the place wherein prescribed ordinances of the priesthood are solemnized but also as a sanctuary where God reveals himself to man. The first such sanctuary on earth was not a building, but the Garden of Eden, where God revealed himself to Adam and gave him certain ordinances pertaining to exaltation. Mount Moriah where Abraham offered sacrifice, the site of the burning bush where God spoke to Moses, and Mount Sinai where Moses communed with God could be classified as sanctuaries. (See James E. Talmage, *The House of the Lord*, pp. 15–16.) There was the Mount of Transfiguration, where the keys of the sealing power were bestowed upon Peter, James, and John by the Prophet Elijah, and in latter days, the Sacred Grove near Palmyra where Joseph Smith received his First Vision. Elder Bruce R. McConkie reports that "endowments . . . following the latter-day exodus, were first given on Ensign Peak" in the Great Salt Lake Valley. (*Mormon Doctrine*, p. 780.) These could also be classified as sanctuaries.

The people of Israel were distinguished among the nations as the builders of sanctuaries to the name of the living God. No sooner had they escaped from the environment of Egyptian idolatry than they were commanded by the Lord to build a tabernacle wherein Jehovah might manifest himself. Though the tabernacle was but a tent, it was made of the best, the most prized, and the costliest materials the people possessed. It was in every respect the best the people had to give, and Jehovah respected their sacrifice by his divine acceptance. (See James E. Talmage, *The House of the Lord*, pp. 2–3.) The Lord "commanded Moses that he should build a tabernacle . . . that those ordinances might be revealed which had been hid from before the world was." (D&C 124:38.) This portable tabernacle was an interesting engineering accomplishment and was completed within one year from the time the children of Israel departed from Egypt.

The first temple building of which we have biblical record is the temple of Solomon built in Jerusalem. The inner structure of Solomon's temple was in arrangement and proportion practically identical to the earlier tabernacle mentioned above. In the temple the dimensions of the Holy of Holies, the Holy Place, and the porch were exactly double those of the corresponding parts of the tabernacle. Construction began on Solomon's temple in the fourth year of his reign and was dedicated in the twelfth, about 1005 B.C. The finest woods available to the known world and the most skilled craftsmen were used. Precious metals, fine linens, and other costly materials made it a structure of renown. Three thousand, three hundred overseers were involved in the construction, giving us an insight into the magnitude of the project.

Even prior to Solomon's death the decline of Israel began, resulting in the deterioration of the temple and finally in its desecration; Shishak, king of Egypt, captured Jerusalem and took away the treasures of Solomon's temple. Deterioration continued through the centuries, and finally in 588 B.C., during the siege of Jerusalem by King Nebuchadnezzar of Babylon, the temple was destroyed by fire. Under the friendly rule of the Persian Empire, the Jews were permitted to return to Jerusalem and restore the temple, which restoration was completed in 515 B.C. It then became known as the temple of Zerubbabel. While this temple was inferior to Solomon's in richness of finish and furnishings, it was the best the people could build and was accepted by the Lord. Time took its toll on this temple, and in 16 B.C. Herod commenced the reconstruction of the decaying temple of Zerubbabel. Many incidents in the earthly life of the

Savior are associated with the temple of Herod. In the year A.D. 70 the temple was utterly destroyed by fire in connection with the capture of Jerusalem by the Romans. (See James E. Talmage, ''Sanctuaries in Earlier Dispensations,'' *The House of the Lord*; and Josephus, *The Wars of the Jews*.)

In the land of Nephi in the Americas, Nephi built a temple about 570 B.C. ''And I did construct it after the manner of the temple of Solomon save it were not built of so many precious things; for they were not to be found upon the land. But the manner of the construction was like unto the temple of Solomon; and the workmanship thereof was exceeding fine.'' (2 Nephi 5:16.) About 124 B.C. King Benjamin invited all the people to hear his words at the temple in Zarahemla. At the visit of Christ to America, the record speaks of a temple in the land of Bountiful. Helaman wrote of ''their building of temples, and of synagogues and their sanctuaries.'' (Helaman 3:14.) It appears there were many temples built in ancient America. The design of the temples built by those who were righteous would presumably have been patterned after the temple of Solomon, as was the temple built by Nephi. The dark ages of history in both the eastern and western hemispheres were a time when the Spirit of the Lord was taken from the earth and when temples of the Lord fell into misuse and disrepair. The righteous of the Lord's chosen people are almost always commanded to build temples unto the Lord devoted to sacred rites and ordinances, not only in former dispensations but today as well; but when the people fall into unrighteousness the temples lose their sanctity and become empty shells and only reminders of their former glory.

''The inspired erection and proper use of temples is one of the great evidences of the divinity of the Lord's work. Without revelation they can neither be built nor used. Where there are temples, with the spirit of revelation resting upon those who administer therein, there the Lord's people will be found; where these are not, the Church and kingdom and the truth of Heaven are not.'' (Bruce R. McConkie, *Mormon Doctrine*, p. 781; Revelation 21–22.)

NAUVOO TEMPLE

We thank thee that thou has given us strength to accomplish the charges delivered by thee. Thou hast seen our labors and exertions to accomplish this purpose. By the authority of the Holy Priesthood now we offer this building as a sanctuary to thy worthy name. We ask thee to take the guardianship into thy hands and grant thy Spirit shall dwell here and may all feel a sacred influence on their hearts that His hand has helped this work.

◆

From the dedicatory prayer by Orson Hyde
May 1, 1846

2

Temples of the Latter Days

◆

Having considered temples of former dispensations, let us now consider temples of the latter days. In 1833 the Lord instructed the Saints to build a temple in Kirtland, Ohio, where they had gathered. (See D&C 88:119.) Eliza R. Snow recorded: "At that time the Saints were few in number, and most of them very poor. . . . With very little capital except brain, bone and sinew, combined with unwavering trust in God, men, women, and even children, worked with their might . . . living as abstemiously as possible, so that every cent might be appropriated to the grand object, while their energies were stimulated by the prospect of participating in the blessing of a house built by the direction of the Most High, and accepted by him." (Cited in Edward W. Tullidge, *Life of Joseph the Prophet*, pp. 187, 189.)

The Kirtland Temple was dedicated on March 27, 1836. On that occasion, with 416 members present, wonderful manifestations occurred.

> Brother George A. Smith arose and began to prophesy, when a noise was heard like the sound of a rushing mighty wind, which filled the Temple, and all the congregation simultaneously arose, being moved upon by an invisible power; many began to speak in tongues and prophesy; others saw glorious visions; and I beheld the Temple was filled with angels, which fact I declared to the congregation. The people of the neighborhood came running together (hearing an unusual sound within and seeing a bright light like a pillar of fire resting upon the Temple), and were astonished at what was taking place. This continued until the meeting closed at eleven p.m. (Joseph Smith, *HC* 2:428.)

The following Sunday manifestations and visitations of even greater significance were received. Joseph Smith and Oliver Cowdery "saw the Lord standing upon the breastwork of the pulpit" in the temple. The Lord said: "For behold, I have accepted this house, and my name shall be here; and I will manifest myself to my people in mercy in this house. Yea, I will appear unto my servants, and speak unto them with mine own voice, if my people will keep my commandments, and do not pollute this holy house. Yea the hearts of thousands and tens of thousands shall greatly rejoice in consequence of the blessings which shall be poured out, and the endowment with which my servants have been endowed in this house.'' (D&C 110:7–9.)

Then Moses appeared and committed to Joseph Smith and Oliver Cowdery the keys of the gathering of Israel. Elias appeared and committed to them the dispensation of the gospel of Abraham. Elijah appeared and bestowed upon them the keys of the sealing power to bind in heaven that which is bound on earth. Thus ''the keys of this dispensation [were] committed into [their] hands.'' (D&C 110:16.) The purpose for which the building had been constructed was fulfilled. This was one of the most important occasions in the dispensation of the fulness of times.

As severe persecution increased, a general exodus of the Saints resulted. Within two years of the dedication, the temple fell into the hands of their persecutors. It became apparent the Lord had instructed the Saints to build the temple for the express purpose of committing the keys of this dispensation so that the building of his kingdom on earth might go forth.

On January 9, 1841, the Lord instructed the Saints to build a temple in Nauvoo, Illinois. The cornerstone of this temple was laid April 6, 1841. It was ''erected by the people, who contributed liberally both through tithes and free will offerings of money and labor. Most of the work was done by men who tithed themselves as to time, and devoted . . . at least one day in ten to labor on the temple.'' (HC 4:517.) Eleven months following the martyrdom of Joseph and Hyrum Smith the capstone was laid, on May 24, 1845, and Brigham Young declared: ''The last stone is laid upon the Temple, and I pray the Almighty in the name of Jesus to defend us in this place, and sustain us until the Temple is finished and [we] have all got our endowments.'' (Historical Record 8:870.)

In the face of heavy persecution the Saints completed the construction of the temple even after many had left the area and were headed west. However, before leaving, the Saints received their sacred endowments. The temple was dedicated under difficult circumstances created by angry mobs on April 30, 1846. By September 1846 the Nauvoo Temple was in the hands of the mob and two years later was destroyed by fire. The Saints fulfilled the Lord's commandment and received the endowment the Lord had promised, which helped prepare them to withstand the hardships they were yet to suffer.

Their trek from Nauvoo to the Great Salt Lake Valley is a history of hardship, difficulties, and suffering which contributed stories of courage, faith, and devotion to the saga of the West. Within four days after the arrival of the first wagon train, Brigham Young selected a ten-acre plot for a house of the Lord, demonstrating the Saints' commitment and dedication to temple building. Construction on the Salt Lake Temple began in 1853. The foundations initially were made of sandstone and were completed in 1857. When Johnston's Army became a threat to the settlements of the Saints during the Utah War, to avoid desecration of the property they covered the foundations with dirt so that the area appeared as a plowed field. When the crisis was over, they replaced the sandstone foundations with solid granite blocks eight feet thick because, as President Brigham Young explained, he wanted the temple to stand through the Millennium. Despite the poverty of the people in very trying times, the work progressed and the building was dedicated on April 6, 1893.

The first temple dedicated in the West was at St. George, next at Logan, then Manti, then the Salt Lake Temple—all in Utah—and so on until today many temples dot the land. The great work of the Millennium will be temple and genealogical service. At the end of the Millennium the earth will be celestialized, the purpose of temples will have been satisfied, and temples will no longer be needed. John the Revelator saw the celestial kingdom and wrote: "And I saw no temple therein: for the Lord God Almighty and the Lamb are the temple of it." (Revelation 21:22.)

ST. GEORGE TEMPLE

We implore thy blessings upon the various congregations of thy people who may assemble in this house from time to time, both in their incomings and their outgoings, and may thy blessing and thy Spirit dwell herein and rest upon them for their comfort and edification, and abide richly in their hearts, that they may learn further of thy ways and walk in thy paths.

◆

From the dedicatory prayer by
Daniel H. Wells
April 6, 1877

3

Jesus and the Temple in His Day

◆

At the time of the birth of the Savior, construction on the temple of Herod in Jerusalem had been in process for sixteen years. Construction continued beyond that time for sixty-three more years. This edifice was similar to the two temples that preceded it on the same location—the temple of Solomon and the temple of Zerubbabel—although its exterior was much more elaborate than the latter. Following the first eighteen months of construction, the sacred operations of the temple were not interrupted even though work was continuous in improving the exterior and in building surrounding courts and ancillary buildings.

It was in this setting that Joseph and Mary brought the infant Jesus to the temple forty days after his birth. It was customary that parents bring their firstborn male to the temple for presentation to the Lord. Simeon, a righteous and devout Israelite living in Jerusalem, had gained a promise from the Holy Ghost that he should not see death until he had looked upon the Son of God in the flesh. Prompted by the Spirit, he visited the temple the day that Joseph and Mary brought Jesus there. He recognized the child as the promised Messiah, took him reverently in his arms, and eloquently expressed an inspired prayer of thanksgiving to his Father in Heaven, closing with the following words: "Lord, now lettest thou thy servant depart in peace, according to thy word: for mine eyes have seen thy salvation, which thou hast prepared before the face of all people; a light to lighten the Gentiles, and the glory of thy people Israel." (Luke 2:29–32.) Then Simeon blessed them, prophesied of the Savior's mission on earth, and advised Mary of the heartbreak she would later suffer.

And the child grew, and waxed strong in spirit, filled with wisdom: and the grace of God was upon him.

Now his parents went to Jerusalem every year at the feast of the passover.

And when he was twelve years old, they went up to Jerusalem after the custom of the feast.

And when they had fulfilled the days, as they returned, the child Jesus tarried behind in Jerusalem; and Joseph and his mother knew not of it.

But they, supposing him to have been in the company, went a day's journey; and they sought him among their kinsfolk and acquaintance.

And when they found him not, they turned back again to Jerusalem, seeking him.

And it came to pass, that after three days they found him in the temple, sitting in the midst of the doctors, both hearing them, and asking them questions.

And all that heard him were astonished at his understanding and answers.

And when [his parents] saw him, they were amazed: and his mother said unto him, Son, why hast thou thus dealt with us? behold, thy father and I have sought thee sorrowing.

And he said unto them, How is it that ye sought me? wist ye not that I must be about my Father's business? . . .

And he went down with them, and came to Nazareth, and was subject unto them. . . .

And Jesus increased in wisdom and stature, and in favour with God and man. (Luke 2:40–52.)

The law of Moses had been supplemented with rules, requirements, and procedures concerning sacrifices and tribute, giving rise to a system of barter and sale within the sacred area of the temple. In the outer courts was maintained an inventory of oxen, sheep, doves, and pigeons that one could purchase for sacrificial purposes. Merchants capitalizing on this opportunity cried aloud the fitness of the victims for a sacrificial offering in an attempt to enrich their coffers.

It was customary for every male to pay one-half shekel each year as a tribute to maintain the temple. Many of those visiting the temple came from areas using a different coinage system than the one used in Jerusalem. The temple would not accept foreign coins; thus, moneychangers set up tables in the temple and carried on a thriving exchange trade. The exuberance they displayed to satisfy their greed resulted in a confusion that desecrated the sanctity of the temple.

Early in the ministry of the Savior he visited the temple. Upon witnessing the confusion and utter disregard for the sanctity of the temple, he improvised a whip of small cords; drove out the moneychangers, upset their tables, and scattered their coins; drove out the merchandisers, freed the oxen and sheep; and with tender regard for the doves and pigeons in their bird cages said, "Take these things hence." To all the greedy traders he thundered forth with a command that made them quail, "Make not my Father's house an house of merchandise." (John 2:16.) His reaction reminded his disciples of the prophetic words of the Psalmist: "The zeal of thine house hath eaten me up." (Psalm 69:9; John 2:17.)

Three years later and just four days before Calvary, the Savior was again filled with indignation at the scene of tumult and confusion he witnessed at the temple. "And Jesus went into the temple of God, and cast out all them that sold and bought in the temple, and overthrew the tables of the moneychangers, and the seats of them that sold doves, and said unto them, It is written, My house shall be called the house of prayer; but ye have made it a den of thieves." (Matthew 21:12–13.)

Previously he had declared the temple "my Father's house," but on this occasion he declared his Messiahship by designating it as "my house." This increased the wrath and indignation of the scribes and priests who had already decreed his death, but they were afraid to touch him for fear of the people.

When the Savior was in Jerusalem, in what more appropriate place could he have taught than in the temple? Some of the precious words he spoke, sermons he gave, and parables he uttered were delivered there. Luke wrote of the Savior's last sojourn in Jerusalem: "And he taught daily in the temple. But the chief priests and the scribes and the chief of the people sought to destroy him, and could not find what they might do: for all the people were very attentive to hear him." (Luke 19:47–48.)

Jesus at first came to the temple to be taught by the Holy Spirit and by the spiritual leaders of the day. Later he came to the temple to teach and to be strengthened in wisdom and understanding by the Holy Spirit, for "he received not of the fulness at first, but continued from grace to grace, until he received a fulness." (D&C 93:13.)

At the crucifixion of the Savior, the veil of the temple was rent to symbolize the spiritual deterioration to which the temple had fallen prey and to mark the ending of an era when God dwelt in his holy house.

Commenting on a remark made by one of the disciples, Jesus had said, "Seest thou these great buildings? there shall not be left one stone upon another, that shall not be thrown down." (Mark 13:2.) In A.D. 70 "this dire prediction . . . found its literal fulfillment. In the great conflict with the legions under Titus, many of the Jews had taken refuge within the Temple courts. . . . But the protecting presence of Jehovah had long since departed therefrom and Israel was left a prey to the foe. Though Titus would have spared the Temple, his legionaries, maddened by the lust of conflict, started the conflagration and everything that could be burned was burned." (James E. Talmage, *Jesus the Christ*, p. 568.)

LOGAN TEMPLE

And, as all wisdom dwells with thee, and, as
all light, truth, and intelligence flow from thee,
we humbly seek unto thee for thy learning
under thy guidance, direction, and inspiration,
as thou didst ordain the laws of the universe,
and art the Creator and Sustainer of worlds,
and the Regulator of their times and seasons,
we ask that in this house a more full knowledge of thee and thy laws may be developed.

◆

From the dedicatory prayer by John Taylor
May 17–19, 1884

4

The Use of Temples
Through the Ages

◆

The first biblical reference to an edifice designed for temple use was the portable tabernacle used by the children of Israel. The tabernacle was within an enclosure seventy-five feet wide and one hundred and fifty feet long encompassed by canvas walls. The east half of the enclosure was an assembly area with an altar for burnt offerings; a laver, which was a brass vessel set upon a pedestal for the priests to use for ceremonial washing of their hands and feet; and pots for incense to symbolize prayer rising from earth to heaven. Here is where the offering of sacrifices took place in compliance with the sacrificial details given to the children of Israel for the Mosaic dispensation.

The west half of the enclosure, which was separated from the east half by a partition, encompassed the tabernacle itself, a tent structure forty-five feet by fifteen feet. The east two-thirds of the tabernacle was known as the Holy Place and the west third as the Holy of Holies. The veil of the temple was located between the two rooms. In the Holy of Holies the mercy seat rested upon the Ark of the Covenant, which contained artifacts symbolic of the Israelites' special experiences with the Lord. At the sides of the seat were cherubim with spread wings offering a covering for the mercy seat. All of this was either in solid gold or overlaid in gold. The furnishings and coverings were made of the finest materials and were the very best the people had to offer. This was the place where the Lord would manifest himself to his chosen people.

Just as on Mount Sinai a cloud had shrouded the temporary abiding place of God, so it was that a cloud covered the tent of the congregation and the glory of the Lord filled the tabernacle. When the cloud was taken up from over the tabernacle, the children of Israel went onward in their journeys, but if the cloud was not taken up they did not travel: "The cloud of the Lord was upon the tabernacle by day, and fire was on it by night, in the sight of all the house of Israel, throughout all their journeys." (Exodus 40:34–38.)

> The all-pervading and all-controlling thought in the erection of this portable sanctuary was that of expressing the close association between Jehovah and His people. The people were to consider themselves specifically the people of God, and amongst them should be His dwelling, surpassing in a transcendent degree the presence of the gods of wood and stone housed among the idolatrous nations with whom Israel had to contend. This thought was expressed in the earliest commandment respecting the building of the Tabernacle: "And let them make a sanctuary; that I may dwell among them." (James E. Talmage, *The House of the Lord*, p. 23.)

As noted, the dimensions of the temple of Solomon were twice that of the tabernacle, which increased the floor space fourfold. Within the court a baptismal font was placed on the backs of twelve life-size oxen representing the twelve tribes of Israel. The ordinances of baptism and sacrifice continued in Solomon's temple, but the higher ordinances of the Melchizedek Priesthood would have been administered rarely, because the higher priesthood was held only by certain prophets from Moses until the time of Christ.

"The offering of sacrifices as a generally practiced ordinance of the gospel ended with the sacrifice of Christ; the sacrament became the newly established ordinance which served the same purpose that sacrifices had theretofore served." (Bruce R. McConkie, *Mormon Doctrine*, p. 665.) Nevertheless, sacrifice would have continued in the temple of Herod because the temple was under the control of those who did not believe that Christ was the Messiah. Temple work for the dead was instituted among the Saints following the crucifixion of Christ, as evidenced by the words of the Apostle Paul in 1 Corinthians 15:29 and by the receipt of the keys of the sealing power by Peter, James, and John from the prophet Elijah. (Matthew 17:3.)

The temple at Kirtland, Ohio, was patterned after neither the tabernacle nor Solomon's temple.

> The first temple of modern times was in a measure incomplete as compared with the holy houses of later construction. The fact was doubtless known to the Lord, though wisely hidden from common knowledge, that the Kirtland Temple would serve but for the beginning of the re-establishment of those distinctive ordinances for which

temples are essential. Even as the Tabernacle of old was but an inferior type of what would follow, designed for temporary use under special conditions, so the earlier temples of the latter-day dispensation, specifically those of Kirtland and Nauvoo, were but temporary Houses of the Lord, destined to serve for short periods only as sanctuaries. (James E. Talmage, *The House of the Lord*, pp. 93–94.)

The Kirtland Temple served as a sacred gathering place where the Lord could restore the various keys for the dispensation of the fulness of times to enable the plan of salvation to blossom as had been intended from before the world began. Partial endowments were given to Church leaders in this temple, specifically consisting of what we now refer to as initiatory ordinances.

The Nauvoo Temple had its purpose and was designed accordingly. In the basement was a replica of the baptismal font of Solomon's temple. Here it was that the ordinances of baptism for the dead took place. Prior to its availability, baptisms for the dead were performed in the Mississippi River starting in 1841. Here in the Nauvoo Temple also ordinances of the endowment were given to worthy members. These ordinances bolstered their commitment and dedication to withstand the hardships ahead.

The Salt Lake Temple and all other subsequently designed temples of the Church, as well as the temple in Nauvoo, have been designed to accommodate the giving of the full endowment to Church members and to enable them to perform all necessary ordinances for the salvation of their deceased ancestors. The construction of the Salt Lake Temple represented the finest artisanship and the best materials that the members could give, with the intent that it should stand throughout the Millennium. Subsequent temples have been constructed to an equivalent standard of excellence.

Now is the day when the promises made by the Lord to Abraham are being fulfilled, that Abraham's seed should bear the Lord's ministry and priesthood unto all nations. To do so requires the use of temples. Instead of requiring members to gather in one place, as has been done in the past, or to come from distant lands to the temples, the Lord is making temples available to them in their own lands, all of which is preparatory to the day of the Savior's second coming.

MANTI TEMPLE

When thy sons and daughters shall desire to plight their faith with
each other unto thee in a covenant of everlasting life and shall
obtain admittance here in thy holy courts, then O Lord, be pleased
to accept their offerings; sanctify them, that they may be clean
from all unrighteousness; clothe thy servants with the habiliments
of the Priesthood, and here at the shrine of thy love seal them thine
by thy Holy Spirit of Promise until the day of their redemption, the
resurrection of their bodies, as purchased by the blood of Christ
thy Son. May this holy temple be to them as one of the gates of
heaven, opening into the straight and narrow path that leads to
endless lives and eternal dominion.

◆

From the dedicatory prayer by
Wilford Woodruff
May 17, 1888

5

Gathering the People of God

◆

Joseph Smith posed the question, "What was the object of gathering the Jews? Or the people of God in any age of the world?" And then he answered his own questions by explaining the purpose of temples:

> The main object was to build unto the Lord a house whereby He could reveal unto His people the ordinances of His house and the glories of His kingdom, and teach the people the way of salvation; for there are certain ordinances and principles that, when they are taught and practiced, must be done in a place or house built for that purpose. . . . It is for the same purpose that God gathers His people in the last days, to build unto the Lord a house to prepare them for the ordinances and endowments, washings and anointings, etc. (*HC* 5:423–24.)

This was the reason why Jesus said unto the Jews, "How often would I have gathered thy children together, even as a hen gathereth her chickens under her wings, and ye would not!" (Matthew 23:37.)

For many years, beginning with the organization of the Church, converts were encouraged to come to Zion and build it up as a center place. Many came from various nations of the world. This enabled center places to be established in the western United States, where the Saints gained sufficient strength and numbers to build and use temples for their eternal salvation. Prior to World War II, instructions were given by the First Presidency for Saints to remain thereafter in the communities in which they resided and to build the Church in their own areas. Thus branches, wards, and stakes grew stronger in various locations throughout the world; and soon there were many stakes, sufficient to support temples in many locations where members could receive their temple blessings without traveling great distances. Thus temple blessings have become more available now to members in their own lands and in their own areas than ever before.

Of the purpose of temples, President John Taylor said:

When Elijah the prophet appeared to Joseph Smith he committed to him the keys of this dispensation; and hence we are at work building Temples; but some of us hardly know why. . . . There are ordinances associated behind these things that go back into eternity; and forward into eternity; that are the offspring of God, that are intended for the welfare, the happiness and exaltation of mankind; for those who are living and for those that are dead and for those that will live hereafter, pertaining both to our progenitors and our posterity. (*JD* 21:95.)

The ordinances to which the prophets refer constitute the temple endowment. "Your endowment is, to receive all those ordinances in the House of the Lord, which are necessary for you, after you have departed this life, to enable you to walk back to the presence of the Father, passing the angels who stand as sentinels, being enabled to give them the key words, the signs and tokens, pertaining to the Holy Priesthood, and gain your eternal exaltation in spite of earth and hell." (Brigham Young, *JD* 2:31.) "The building of Temples, places in which the ordinances of salvation are administered, is necessary to carry out the plan of redemption." (Brigham Young, *JD* 13:262.)

The question is frequently asked "Can we not be saved without going through with all those ordinances, etc?" I would answer, No, not the fullness of salvation. Jesus said, "There are many mansions in my Father's house, and I will go and prepare a place for you." *House* here named should have been translated kingdom; and any person who is exalted to the highest mansion has to abide a celestial law, and the whole law too. . . .

I have tried for a number of years to get the minds of the Saints prepared to receive the things of God; but we frequently see some of them, after suffering all they have for the work of God, will fly to pieces like glass as soon as anything comes that is contrary to their traditions: they cannot stand the fire at all. How many will be able to abide a celestial law, and go through and receive their exaltation, I am unable to say, as many are called, but few are chosen. (Joseph Smith, *HC* 6:184–85.)

President Joseph Fielding Smith wrote:

Elijah came to restore to the earth . . . the fulness of the power of priesthood. This priesthood holds the keys of binding and sealing on earth and in heaven of all the ordinances and principles pertaining to the salvation of man, that they may thus become valid in the celestial kingdom of God. . . . This power effects and vitalizes every ordinance performed by duly commissioned officers holding divine power on the earth.

It is by virtue of this authority that ordinances are performed in the temples for both the living and the dead. It is the power which unites for eternity husbands and wives, when they enter into marriage according to the eternal plan. It is the authority by which parents obtain the claim of parenthood, concerning their children, through all eternity and not only for time, which makes eternal the family in the kingdom of God. (*Doctrines of Salvation* 2:117.)

This gathering of Saints and the restoration of these precious priesthood powers and temple ordinances are an important part of that which the Apostle Paul made reference to nearly two thousand years ago in his epistle to the Ephesian Saints: "That in the dispensation of the fulness of times he might gather together in one all things in Christ, both which are in heaven, and which are on earth." (Ephesians 1:10.)

SALT LAKE TEMPLE

When thy people . . . are oppressed and in trouble, surrounded by difficulties or assailed by
temptation and shall turn their faces towards
this thy holy house and ask thee for deliverance, for help, for thy power to be extended
in their behalf, we beseech thee, to look down
from thy holy habitation in mercy and tender
compassion upon them and listen to their cries.

◆

From the dedicatory prayer by
Wilford Woodruff
April 6–24, 1893

6
Temple Ordinances— Their Origin and Use

◆

Where did the temple ordinances originate? In a revelation given to the Prophet Joseph Smith on January 19, 1841, the Lord commanded the Saints to build a temple in Nauvoo, Illinois, and then said: "Let this house be built unto my name, that I may reveal mine ordinances therein unto my people; for I deign to reveal unto my church things which have been kept hid from before the foundation of the world, things that pertain to the dispensation of the fulness of times. And I will show unto my servant Joseph all things pertaining to this house, and the priesthood thereof, and the place whereon it shall be built." (D&C 124:40–42.)

How does the Lord keep these ordinances hidden and from whom? The temple ordinances are sacred and should not be flaunted before the world. We want to share the temple blessings with all of God's children, but they must prepare themselves first. We are taught in the temple to maintain their confidentiality. This Alma explained to Zeezrom:

> It is given unto many to know the mysteries of God; nevertheless they are laid under a strict command that they shall not impart only according to that portion of his word which he doth grant unto the children of men, according to the heed and diligence which they give unto him.
>
> And therefore, he that will harden his heart, the same receiveth the lesser portion of the word; and he that will not harden his heart, to him is given the greater portion of the word, until it is given unto him to know the mysteries of God until he knows them in full.
>
> And they that will harden their hearts, to them is given the lesser portion of the word until they know nothing concerning his mysteries; and then they are taken captive by the devil, and led by his will down to destruction. Now this is what is meant by the chains of hell. (Alma 12:9–11.)

In this manner the Lord has kept an understanding of these ordinances hidden from the eyes of the world but has shared them with worthy Saints. The scripture does not mean that the Lord had never given them to any man before he gave them to the Prophet Joseph.

> These revelations, which are reserved for and taught only to the faithful Church members in sacred temples, constitute what are called the "mysteries of Godliness." The Lord said He had given to Joseph "the keys of the mysteries, and the revelations which are sealed. . . ." (D&C 28:7.) As a reward to the faithful, the Lord promised: "And to them will I reveal all mysteries, yea, all the hidden mysteries of my kingdom from days of old. . . . " (D&C 76:7.) In this sense, then, a mystery may be defined as a truth which cannot be known except by revelation. (Harold B. Lee, *Ye Are the Light of the World*, pp. 210–11.)

The Prophet Joseph, having received knowledge of the ordinances of the endowment through revelation, taught certain Church leaders the details of the endowment on May 4, 1842.

> I spent the day in the upper part of the store, that is in my private office . . . in council with [several early Church leaders], instructing them in the principles and order of the Priesthood, attending to washings, anointings, endowments and the communication of keys pertaining to the Aaronic Priesthood, and so on to the highest order of the Melchizedek Priesthood, setting forth the order pertaining to the Ancient of Days, and all those plans and principles by which any one is enabled to secure the fulness of those blessings which have been prepared for the Church of the Firstborn, and come up and abide in the presence of the Eloheim in the eternal worlds. (*Teachings of the Prophet Joseph Smith*, p. 237.)

This precious endowment was not intended for this dispensation only. "Adam and his posterity were commanded by God to be baptized, to receive the Holy Ghost, and to enter into the order of the Son of God. To enter into the order of the Son of God is the equivalent . . . of entering into the fullness of the Melchizedek Priesthood, which is only received in the house of the Lord. . . . Today we would say they went to the house of the Lord and received their blessings." (Ezra Taft Benson, "What I Hope You Will Teach Your Children About the Temple," *Ensign*, August 1985, pp. 8–9.)"And the Lord ordained Noah after his own Order" (Moses 8:19); Noah would thus have been responsible for transmitting the authority of the priesthood and the knowledge of the temple ordinances and blessings beyond the flood.

The Lord also honored Melchizedek who held the Holy Priesthood after the Order of the Son of God, by changing the name of the order to the Melchizedek Priesthood to avoid the too frequent use of the name of Deity. Josephus, the renowned historian, wrote, ''(Melchizedek) the Righteous King, . . . first built a temple, (there,) and called the city Jerusalem, which was formerly called Salem.'' (Josephus, *Complete Works*, p. 588.) Abraham paid tithes to Melchizedek and received the priesthood under his hands. We may assume that Melchizedek, as a holder of the Melchizedek Priesthood and builder of a temple, received his temple blessings—as one might also infer from reading Abraham 1:2–4.

Moses received the Melchizedek Priesthood from his father-in-law, Jethro, who was a Midianite. The Midianites were descendants of Abraham. Under instructions from the Lord, the children of Israel built the tabernacle of the congregation, which was portable and was transported from place to place as they wandered about in the Sinai Desert for forty years. It was designed to enable the children of Israel to perform priesthood ordinances. We do not know how many of the children of Israel received their Melchizedek Priesthood blessings; but we do know that Moses ''sought diligently to sanctify his people that they might behold the face of God [as did Moses]; but they hardened their hearts and could not endure his presence; therefore, the Lord in his wrath, for his anger was kindled against them, swore that they should not enter into his rest while in the wilderness, which rest is the fulness of his glory. Therefore he took Moses out of their midst, and the Holy Priesthood also.'' (D&C 84:23–25.) The Aaronic Priesthood continued, but the blessings and ordinances of the higher priesthood were not available to them. From that time onward only certain Old Testament prophets held the Melchizedek Priesthood. (See Bruce R. McConkie, *Mormon Doctrine*, p. 477.) The last Old Testament prophet to hold the keys of the sealing power was Elijah, who bestowed that power and authority upon Peter, James, and John on the Mount of Transfiguration.

In these days of restoration—in this the dispensation of the fulness of times—these precious and sacred priesthood ordinances and the priesthood authority to administer them have been restored. We have been permitted to build temples in lands throughout the world where worthy members can come and receive these same sacred ordinances. In this way we prepare ourselves to enter into the presence of the Lord and gain our eternal salvation, just as the first man, Adam, did. How blessed we are.

HAWAII TEMPLE

May thy peace ever abide in this holy building, that all who come here may partake of
the spirit of peace, and of the sweet and heavenly influence that thy Saints have experienced
in other temples. . . . May all who come upon
the grounds which surround this temple, in the
years to come, whether members of the Church
of Christ or not, feel the sweet and peaceful
influence of this blessed and hallowed spot.

◆

From the dedicatory prayer by
Heber J. Grant
November 27, 1919

7

The House of the Lord

◆

The words "Holiness to the Lord—The House of the Lord" are cast in stone on each temple of The Church of Jesus Christ of Latter-day Saints. The buildings are built by contributions from members. They have been dedicated and presented to the Lord as his House. Each temple is of the finest workmanship available and of the best material that can be obtained, for nothing is too good for the Lord.

A temple is a special place. Temples of The Church of Jesus Christ of Latter-day Saints are Christ centered. Paintings and murals on the walls depict events in the life of the Savior. The ordinances performed therein pertain to Christ and our relationship with him. We believe in Christ. He is our God and our king. While we pray to God the Father, we hold Christ in adoration and revere him as our creator and redeemer. He has given us the fulness of his gospel. We are the custodians of the fulness of the gospel of Jesus Christ. We strive to live our lives in conformity to his gospel.

The first building of The Church of Jesus Christ of Latter-day Saints was not a chapel, but a temple built in Kirtland, Ohio. The Lord commanded the Saints to construct the temple and gave instructions regarding its design. Our priorities regarding temples have not changed, nor will they.

Temples are sacred buildings—the most important buildings we have in the Church. The ordinances performed therein are not secret. We want everyone to receive them, but to do so they must be properly prepared. When a person is prepared through understanding, accepting, and living the gospel of Jesus Christ, he is welcome to come to the temple. It would be pleasing to us if all prepared themselves and came. We want to share this wonderful blessing with all mankind. However, the temple ordinances are sacred. They should not be exposed to those who are not ready to receive them, else the ordinances would lose their sacredness and it would be to the condemnation of those who might ridicule and hold them in derision.

The temple has a fourfold purpose:

(1) The Lord instructed the Saints, preparatory to the c ̲ ̲ ̲ ̲ uc-tion of the temple in Nauvoo, to "build a house to [his] name, for the Most High to dwell therein. For there is not a place found on earth that he may come to and restore again that which was lost unto you, or which he hath taken away, even the fulness of the priesthood." (D&C 124:27–28.) This situation was not different from the time in the Savior's ministry when he said, "The foxes have holes, and the birds of the air have nests; but the Son of man hath not where to lay his head." (Matthew 8:20.) So the temple is a place where the Lord can come when he visits the earth. It is a place of communion and revelation and blessings.

Elder John A. Widtsoe explains these blessings:

> It is a great promise that to the temples God will come, and that in them man shall see God. What does this promised communion mean? Does it mean that once in a while God may come into the temples, and that once in a while the pure in heart may see God there; or does it mean the larger thing, that the pure in heart who go into the temples, may, there, by the Spirit of God, always have a wonderfully rich communion with God? I think that is what it means to me and to you and to most of us. We have gone into these holy houses, with our minds freed from the ordinary earthly cares, and have literally felt the presence of God. In this way, the temples are always places where God manifests himself to man and increases his intelligence. A temple is a place of revelation. ("Temple Worship," *Utah Genealogical and Historical Magazine* 12:56.)

(2) From the foundation of the world, the plan of salvation was designed so that every living soul might have the opportunity of hearing and accepting or rejecting the gospel. To accommodate those who have died without the opportunity to hear and receive the gospel in this life, that same gospel of Jesus Christ is being taught to them in the spirit world. Not only does God's plan encompass teaching everyone born on this earth the gospel, but it also promises the full benefits to those who accept. This requires that temple blessings be performed on earth in their behalf which will enable them to enter into exaltation in the celestial kingdom of God, and thus receive the full blessings that eternal life has to offer.

The temple is the only place where these saving ordinances can be performed by the living for the dead. These are earthly ordinances that the dead cannot perform for themselves. This gives us opportunity to do for them what they cannot do for themselves. Brigham Young taught that ''we have a work to do just as important in its sphere as the Savior's work was in its sphere. Our fathers cannot be made perfect without us; we cannot be made perfect without them. They have done their work and now sleep. We are now called upon to do ours; which is to be the greatest work man ever performed on the earth.'' (*JD 18:213.*)

(3) The temple is a place where Saints of God are endowed from on high with sacred blessings that strengthen character and build faith, dedication, and commitment. They are taught eternal truths that expand the vision of man and enrich his life. Elder James E. Talmage discussed the meaning of that part of one's temple blessings referred to as the endowment as follows:

> The temple endowment, as administered in modern temples, comprises instruction relating to the significance and sequence of past dispensations, and the importance of the present as the greatest and grandest era in human history. This course of instruction includes a recital of the most prominent events of the creative period, the condition of our first parents in the Garden of Eden, their disobedience and consequent expulsion from that blissful abode, their condition in the lone and dreary world when doomed to live by labor and sweat, the plan of redemption by which the great transgression may be atoned, the period of the great apostasy, the restoration of the Gospel with all its ancient powers and privileges, the absolute and indispensable condition of personal purity and devotion to the right in present life, and a strict compliance with Gospel requirements. . . .
>
> The ordinances of the endowment embody certain obligations on the part of the individual, such as covenant and promise to observe the law of strict virtue and chastity, to be charitable, benevolent, tolerant and pure; to devote both talent and material means to the spread of truth and the uplifting of the race; to maintain devotion to the cause of truth; and to seek in every way to contribute to the great preparation that the earth may be made ready to receive her King,—the Lord Jesus Christ. With the taking of each covenant and the assuming of each obligation a promised blessing is pronounced, contingent upon the faithful observance of the conditions.
>
> No jot, iota, or tittle of the temple rites is otherwise than uplifting and sanctifying. In every detail the endowment ceremony contributes to covenants of morality of life, consecration of person to high ideals, devotion to truth, patriotism to nation, and allegiance to God. (*The House of the Lord*, pp. 83–84.)

President Harold B. Lee explained, "When you enter a holy temple, you are by that course gaining fellowship with the Saints in God's eternal kingdom, where time is no more. In the temples of your God you are endowed not with the rich legacy of worldly treasure, but with a wealth of eternal riches that are above price." ("Enter a Holy Temple," *Improvement Era*, June 1967, p. 144.)

(4) It is only in the temple that we receive the fulness of the priesthood. On January 19, 1841, the Prophet Joseph received the following revelation: "For there is not a place found on earth that he [the Lord] may come to and restore again that which was lost unto you, or which he hath taken away, even the fulness of the priesthood." (D&C 124:28.)

It is in the temple that we enter into the patriarchal order, the order of priesthood that bears the name "the new and everlasting covenant of marriage."

The opportunity the fulness of the priesthood offers was expressed by the Lord when he said, "For therein are the keys of the holy priesthood ordained [set in order], that you may receive honor and glory." (D&C 124:34.) This honor and glory to which he refers is the same of which the Savior spoke when he addressed his twelve Apostles: "In my Father's house are many mansions: if it were not so, I would have told you. I go to prepare a place for you.

"And if I go and prepare a place for you, I will come again, and receive you unto myself; that where I am there ye may be also." (John 14:2–3.)

The glory to which the Lord refers is the celestial glory, which is the glory of the Father. Of it we are instructed: "In the celestial glory there are three heavens or degrees; And in order to attain the highest, a man must enter into this order of the priesthood (meaning the new and everlasting covenant of marriage); And if he does not, he cannot obtain it. He may enter into the other, but that is the end of his kingdom; he cannot have an increase." (D&C 131:1–4.)

"Abraham received promises concerning his seed [posterity], and of the fruit of his loins . . . which were to continue so long as they were in the world; and as touching Abraham and his seed, out of the world they should continue; both in the world and out of the world should they continue as innumerable as the stars; or, if ye were to count the sand upon the seashore ye could not number them." (D&C 132:30.)

Speaking to Joseph Smith and to those faithful members of the Church in all ages and in all places (see D&C 84:34), the Lord continued: ''This promise is yours also, because ye are of Abraham, and the promise was made unto Abraham; and by this law is the continuation of the works of the Father, wherein he glorifieth himself. Go ye, therefore, and do the works of Abraham; enter ye into my law and ye shall be saved. But if ye enter not into my law ye cannot receive the promise of my Father, which he made unto Abraham.'' (D&C 132: 31–33.)

ALBERTA TEMPLE

We especially pray thee, O Father in Heaven, to bless the youth of thy people in Zion and in all the world. Shield them from the adversary and from wicked and designing men. Keep the youth of thy people, O Father, in the straight and narrow path that leads to thee, preserve them from the pitfalls and snares that are laid for their feet. O Father, may our children grow up in the nurture and admonition of the Lord Jesus Christ. Give unto them a testimony of the divinity of this work as thou hast given it unto us, and preserve them in purity and in the truth.

◆

From the dedicatory prayer by
Heber J. Grant
August 26–29, 1923

8

The Significance of Temple Service

◆

Temple ordinances instituted in the heavens before the foundation of the world are for the salvation and exaltation of God's children. It is important that the saving ordinances not be altered or changed, because all of those who will be exalted, from the first man, Adam, to the last, must be saved on the same principles.

Elder H. Burke Peterson, after serving for a year as president of the Jordan River Temple, explained the significance of temple service:

> I believe one of the best-kept secrets in the Church today is that participation in the ordinances of the temple is the most effective classroom for the perfecting of the Saints. It is my belief that participating in the ordinances of the temple is sanctification's most intense experience. . . . Young and old are equally benefited by the opportunity of temple service. Perhaps the young in the midst of life's battles have more need than the old of the sustaining power that comes from participating in the holy activities in the temple. The response of the spirit of man to the ordinances of the House of the Lord stimulates every normal power and activity and helps greatly in the accomplishments of our daily tasks. More joy enters into the daily routine of life, the spiritual visions become clearer, love for our fellowmen increases within our hearts, peace tempers the tempest of life, and we rise to higher levels of thoughts and actions. In time greater success is achieved. Happiness between man and wife and in the family circle is greatly increased. (First Quorum of the Seventy Meeting Address, 20 February 1986.)

In the temple the plan of salvation is depicted, and we learn the answers to the age-old questions that are asked and pondered by people of every nation, race, and tongue: "From where did I come? Why am I here? Where am I going?" In the temple we make sacred covenants with the Lord that relate to principles of honesty, integrity, morality, obedience, and commitment. Elder George F. Richards said:

We who have no other intent than to be faithful in all things do not hesitate making covenants to that end. Every covenant we enter into with the Lord, is for our own good and blessing. If there are any among us who are weak and hesitate, being fearful, lest they might not be able to keep the required covenants of the gospel, they should lean more heavily upon the assistance the Lord has promised . . . when he said, "Come unto me, all ye that labour and are heavy laden, and I will give you rest. Take my yoke upon you, and learn of me; for I am meek and lowly in heart: and ye shall find rest unto your souls. For my yoke is easy, and my burden is light." (Matthew 11:28–30.) ("Admonition," *Improvement Era*, May 1945, p. 243.)

Lorenzo Snow said:

There is but one way by which exaltation and glory can be secured. We have to be baptized for the remission of sins and have hands laid upon us for the reception of the Holy Ghost. These and other ordinances are absolutely necessary for exaltation and glory; and where individuals have lived when the Gospel has not been accessible, these things can be attended to by their friends. We have come into the world now in order to do these things. . . . We cannot lay too great stress upon the importance of this work." (*MS* 57:405.)

When these ordinances are attended to by friends, they are controlled by rules that satisfy laws of privacy and maintain order and integrity in the process.

"It is not only necessary that you should be baptized for your dead," Joseph Smith said, "but you will have to go through all the ordinances for them, the same as you have gone through to save yourselves." (*HC* 6:365.) Vicarious baptisms for the dead sustain God's position of being a just god and no respecter of persons, for the Savior said, "Except a man be born of water and of the Spirit, he cannot enter into the kingdom of God." (John 3:5.) "Every man who wishes to save his father, mother, brothers, sisters and friends, must go through all the ordinances for each one of them separately, the same as for himself." (Joseph Smith, *HC* 6:319.) These ordinances, including the ordinances of sealing, "will not be performed anywhere but in a Temple; neither will children be sealed to their living parents in any other place than a Temple." (Brigham Young, *JD* 16:186.)

Many prophets have emphasized the work for the dead: "It depends upon the living here to erect Temples, that the ordinances for the dead may be attended to, for by and by you will meet your progenitors in the spirit world who never heard the sound of the Gospel. You who are here in Zion have power to be baptized for and to redeem your dead." (Wilford Woodruff, *JD* 17:250.) "We are building temples to the name of the Lord. What are we building them for? That we may enter in and redeem our dead." (*JD* 22:209.) "We have got to enter into those temples and redeem our dead. . . . This is the great work of the last dispensation—the redemption of the living and the dead." (*JD* 21:192, 194.) "One of the great works in this gospel of salvation, devolving upon us as Saints, is to labor in the temples of God for the salvation of our dead." (Heber J. Grant, *CR*, October 1913, p. 87.) "The greatest responsibility in this world that God has laid upon us, is to seek after our dead." (Joseph Smith, *TS* 5:15:616.) And thus the prophets of God have spoken concerning our responsibility to our progenitors in this the last dispensation, which is the dispensation of the fulness of times.

As we accomplish this redeeming service for our ancestors, we are at the same time preparing ourselves for celestial glory. Both are important and essential to the fulfillment of the plan of salvation that a kind and gracious Father has designed for the redemption of his children.

ARIZONA TEMPLE

Accept the dedication of this house, and these grounds, which we have dedicated unto thee by virtue of the Priesthood of the Living God which we hold, and we most earnestly pray that this sacred building may be a place in which thy Son may see fit to manifest Himself and to instruct thy servants, and in which thou shall delight to dwell.

◆

From the dedicatory prayer by
Heber J. Grant
October 23, 1927

9

A Legacy of Sacrifice

◆

Throughout history the Lord has required sacrifice from his chosen people. Following Adam's expulsion from the Garden of Eden, he was instructed to offer as a sacrifice to the Lord a firstling of the flock that was without blemish. The sacrifice was to be in similitude of the atoning sacrifice of the Savior. From Adam to Christ sacrifices were offered to the Lord. The atonement of Christ ended animal sacrifice. "And ye shall offer up unto me no more the shedding of blood," the Lord said. "Yea, your sacrifices and your burnt offerings shall be done away, for I will accept none of your sacrifices and your burnt offerings. And ye shall offer for a sacrifice unto me a broken heart and a contrite spirit." (3 Nephi 9:19–20.)

The Lord instituted the sacrament of the Last Supper just prior to his atonement. Before his crucifixion the offering of sacrifice symbolized his atonement. After his crucifixion partaking of the sacrament was in remembrance of his atoning sacrifice. The atonement of Jesus Christ was the greatest sacrifice that has ever been made or ever will or can be made in the history of man.

Great sacrifices were made by the Saints following the restoration of the gospel and the Church of Jesus Christ. A temple had to be built where the Lord could come to restore the keys of the kingdom. The Lord instructed the Saints to gather in Kirtland, Ohio, their principal purpose being to build a temple. From the day the ground was broken for laying the foundation until its dedication, the work was vigorously pursued. Heber C. Kimball reported, "While we were building the Temple, in Kirtland, we were poor . . . for at that time we were persecuted and were under the necessity of laying upon the floor with our firelocks by our sides to sustain ourselves, as there were mobs gathering all around us to destroy us, and prevent us from building the Temple." (*TS* 6:13:972.) This indeed was a time of sacrifice, for not only did the Saints live under the threat of mob violence but they also lived as frugally as possible so that every cent might be appropriated to the building of the temple.

> But what of the Temple in Nauvoo? By the aid of the sword in one hand, and trowel and hammer in the other, with firearms at hand, and a strong band of police, and the blessings of heaven, the Saints, through hunger, and thirst, and weariness, and watchings, and prayings, . . . completed the Temple, despite the devices of the mob. . . . And then, to save the lives of all the Saints from cruel murder, we moved westward. . . . Of our journey hither, we need say nothing, only, God led us. Of the sufferings of those who were compelled to, and did, leave Nauvoo in the winter of 1846, we need say nothing. Those who experienced it know it, and those who did not, to tell them of it would be like exhibiting a beautiful painting to a blind man. (Brigham Young, *JD* 2:32.)

A careful study of the history of the Great Basin would enable one to understand the difficulties that the Saints underwent during the construction of the Salt Lake Temple from 1853 to 1893. The trek to the remote deserts of western America did not end persecution. Harassment continued, but violence was avoided by the wisdom of level-headed leadership and by inspiration and revelation.

Now we are in a new era. Temple building has expanded until today the fulness of the gospel is available to the Saints in many countries of the world. The resources of the Church that have been and are now being committed to temple building and temple operations can only mean one thing—the Lord is serious about the redemption of the dead. Our sacrifice has moved from welfare and building assessments to the sacrifice of time and expense to come to the temple regularly to redeem our dead.

The Lord said:

> Therefore, verily I say unto you, that your anointings, and your washings, and your baptisms for the dead, and your solemn assemblies, and your memorials for your sacrifices by the sons of Levi, and for your oracles in your most holy places wherein you receive conversations, and your statutes and judgments, for the beginning of the revelations and foundation of Zion, and for the glory, honor, and endowment of all her municipals, are ordained by the ordinance of my holy house, which my people are always commanded to build unto my holy name. (D&C 124:39.)

Having enumerated the things which the Saints were to do in the temple which was to be constructed, the Lord then warned, "And it shall come to pass that if you build a house unto my name, and do not do the things that I say, I will not perform the oath which I make unto you, neither fulfill the promises which ye expect at my hands." (D&C 124:47.) This counsel is as applicable to us today as it was to the Saints in the days of Nauvoo.

Temples have been built today for the express purpose of redeeming the living and the dead. It is unwise that we jeopardize the promises of God through failure to return regularly to the temple to receive promised blessings for the salvation of our dead and to prepare ourselves for celestial glory in the kingdom of God.

IDAHO FALLS TEMPLE

We pray now that thou wilt accept this temple as a freewill offering from thy children, that will be sacred unto thee. We pray that
all that has been accomplished here may be pleasing in thy sight
and that thou wilt be mindful of this structure at all times that it
may be preserved from the fury of the elements and wilt thou, our
Heavenly Father, let thy presence be felt here always, that all who
assemble here may realize that they are thy guests and that this is
thy house.

◆

From the dedicatory prayer by
David O. McKay
September 23–25, 1945

10

Undaunted by Persecution

◆

The dispensation of the fulness of times is distinguished in the ecclesiastical history of God's chosen people by the construction of temples. The adversary is well aware of the role of temples in fulfilling the plan of salvation. The importance of temple ordinances in the latter days was communicated by the Lord in his warning that "if it were not so, the whole earth would be utterly wasted at his coming." (D&C 2:3.) The adversary would be pleased to waste the earth.

Soon after the Church was organized the Lord gave instructions through the Prophet Joseph Smith that a temple should be built in Kirtland, Ohio. Construction began when the Saints were few in number and most of them were very poor. The erection of the temple in Kirtland seemed to increase the hostile opposition to which the Church had been subjected since its organization.

Sidney Rigdon spoke of "those who had wet [the walls] with their tears, in the silent shades of night, while they were praying to the God of heaven to protect them, and stay the unhallowed hands of ruthless spoilers, who had uttered a prophecy, when the foundation was laid, that the walls would never be reared." (*HC* 2:414.)

Elder George A. Smith said, "Persecution raged around us to such an extent that we were obliged to forsake our beautiful Temple, and flee to the State of Missouri." (*JD* 2:216.) The temple soon fell into the hands of the persecutors; nevertheless, it had fulfilled the purpose for which it was built—to enable the keys of the kingdom to be restored. (See D&C 110.)

> The Saints gathered into Nauvoo, labored and toiled to finish the Temple. [Their] enemies at the same time were planning to drive [them] from [their] city and from the United States. . . . In the small settlements in the country the mobs collected, drove [the] brethren from their homes, burned their houses and grain and killed some who could not get out of the way. In the fall [of 1845], the mob collected in the south part of the county and in about two weeks they had burned 200

houses to ashes. The inhabitants had to flee to Nauvoo to save their lives. A great amount of grain and property was destroyed, cattle and hogs were stolen and killed almost without number. Old father Durfee was shot and killed while he was trying to save his property from the flames. Many others died from exposure after being robbed and driven into the wood. Their sufferings were so great that they could not endure it. (*Autobiography of John Pulsipher*, p. 8.)

Elder George A. Smith said about the Nauvoo Temple: "We went to work in Nauvoo and finished the Temple, and had no sooner got it done but we had to leave it to be burned by our enemies; and they then thought that if we were only driven into the wilderness, our sufferings would be so great in the desert that we should all perish, and that would be the end of the matter." (*JD* 2:218–219.)

Opposition to the construction of the Salt Lake Temple was addressed by Elder John A. Widtsoe in 1921:

> There never yet has been a time in the history of the world when temple work has increased without a corresponding increase in opposition to it. Some three or four years after the pioneers came to this valley, President Brigham Young said that it was time to begin the building of a temple; and some of the old timers here will probably remember that thousands of the Saints dreaded the command, because they said, "Just as soon as we lay the cornerstone of a temple, all hell will be turned loose upon us and we will be driven out of the valleys." President Young thought that was true, but that they also would have, if temple work were undertaken, a corresponding increase in power to overcome all evil. Men grow mighty under the results of temple service; women grow strong under it; the community increases in power; until the devil has less influence than he ever had before. The opposition to truth is relatively smaller if the people are engaged actively in the ordinances of the temple. ("Temple Worship," *The Utah Genealogical and Historical Magazine* 12:51.)

When construction began on the Salt Lake Temple someone reminded Brigham Young that "we never began to build a Temple without the bells of hell beginning to ring." Brigham Young, unintimidated, replied, "I want to hear them ring again." (*JD* 8:355.) Even though the Saints had isolated themselves in the mountains of the West, opposition followed them. It wasn't long before Johnston's Army was dispatched from Leavenworth, Kansas, with the slogan Beauty And Booty on their lips as they marched westward. Recorded history tells the outcome and the opposition that rained down against the Saints for many years during the construction of the Salt Lake Temple.

As the tempo of temple building has increased in recent years, so has the opposition to temples and the Church and all it stands for. It seems a barrage has been unleashed. Undaunted and unintimidated, the Saints today stand as did the Saints of earlier days, going about their business quietly and effectively, knowing with Elisah that "they that be with us are more than they that be with them" (2 Kings 6:16) and firm in the promise that "none shall stay them, for . . . the Lord [has so] commanded them." (D&C 1:5.)

While the persecution rages, the Saints proceed to build the kingdom of God by heeding the counsel of the Lord: "And thou shalt declare glad tidings, yea, publish it upon the mountains, and upon every high place, and among every people that thou shalt be permitted to see. And thou shalt do it with all humility, trusting in me, reviling not against revilers. And of tenets thou shalt not talk, but thou shalt declare repentance and faith on the Savior, and remission of sins by baptism, and by fire, yea, even the Holy Ghost." (D&C 19:29–31.)

SWISS TEMPLE

Increase our desire, O Father, to put forth even greater effort towards the consummation of thy purpose to bring to pass the immortality and eternal life of all thy children. This edifice is one more means to aid in bringing about this divine consummation.

◆

From the dedicatory prayer by
David O. McKay
September 11, 1955

11

We Will Build Zion

◆

The prophecy of the Prophet Daniel (Daniel 2:44), together with other holy scriptures, has made it clear that in these latter days God would set up a kingdom that would roll forth to all the world. When the Saints arrived in the Great Salt Lake Valley, following their trek across the plains and mountains of western America, the Brethren were well aware of the role of the restored Church in fulfilling this prophecy. First they must build Zion, then they must build the world. How could such a bold challenge be fulfilled by a small group of people who had been persecuted, driven time and again from their homes, and taken refuge in the remote deserts of western America?

Soon after their arrival President Brigham Young sent contingencies of Saints to the more fertile areas of the Intermountain West. This enabled the members to establish themselves and gave opportunity for a livelihood and an economic base to support themselves and others who were to follow. As these communities grew and expanded, the building of temples began. Six years following their arrival, construction began on the Salt Lake Temple. Then it was St. George, Logan, and Manti in Utah; and later Hawaii; Cardston, Alberta; Mesa, Arizona; and Idaho Falls, Idaho. These temples were important in the process of building the Zion of which Brigham Young spoke, for Zion is where the pure in heart dwell.

Elder John A. Widtsoe wrote:

> Spiritual power is generated within temple walls, and sent out to bless the world. Light from the house of the Lord illumines every home within the Church fitted for its reception by participation in temple privileges. . . . Every home penetrated by the temple spirit enlightens, cheers, and comforts every member of the household. The peace we covet is found in such homes. Indeed, when temples are on earth, the whole world shares measurably in the issuing light; when absent, the hearts of men become heavy, as if they said, with the people of Enoch's day, "Zion is fled."

Temples are for the benefit and enlightenment of the members of the Church. In them are revealed the keys of the Priesthood, and there power is given men "from on high" to meet the many issues of life. There men may commune with the forces of heaven, until doubt and questioning are replaced by knowledge and certainty. The ordinances and rituals of the temple, profoundly meaningful, set forth completely and comprehensively the truths of life, explain the mystery of existence, and make the Gospel more understandable. Those who have received with open hearts the blessings of the temple go out with increased power and a new understanding of life's problems. ("The House of the Lord," *Improvement Era*, April 1936, p. 228.)

Elder George F. Richards said, "To the careful observer, doubtful as to the value of temple work, the abundant evidences of spiritual growth of those who engage in it is most convincing. There is a calm and sweet serenity about them which is indeed heavenly." ("Latter-day Temples," *Improvement Era*, May 1930, p. 471.)

Those who have repeatedly witnessed the effect of temple construction and operation in various areas have recognized the leavening influence and the spiritual uplift that settles upon the community it serves. In addition to temples, the early Saints built meetinghouses where they worshipped God and learned about him. Also schools were established, for they believed that "the glory of God is intelligence" (D&C 93:36) and that "whatever principle of intelligence we attain unto in this life, it will rise with us in the resurrection." (D&C 130:18.) The Lord blessed them and they grew in faith, wisdom, knowledge, and understanding.

About the time of the Second World War and thereafter, some of the posterity of these pioneers accepted job opportunities in various areas of the world. To a considerable degree they became the nucleus of leadership for building congregations of faithful Saints throughout the United States. Missionary labors expanded dramatically throughout the world. The day of the Lamanites arrived (see D&C 3:18–20), and congregations of faithful Latter-day Saints multiplied in Latin America and in many other nations as well.

Moses had committed the keys of the gathering of Israel in the Kirtland Temple. (See D&C 110:11.) Initially, the gathering was basically from the western European countries, a migration of Saints who came to America to build Zion. Later the gathering continued, but in their own lands. Elias had also appeared in the Kirtland Temple and "committed the dispensation of the gospel of Abraham, saying that in us and our seed all generations after us should be blessed." (D&C 110:12.) The world is strengthened by the influence for good disseminated by those who have received the fulness of the gospel as it is taken to the nations of the world. Those who have the fulness of the gospel have the fulness of the Melchizedek Priesthood, which can only be received in a temple of the Lord.

In recent years temple construction has expanded until we have temples in every nation and in every area where we have sufficient members to sustain one. This is the day spoken of by Nephi: "And it came to pass that I, Nephi, beheld the power of the Lamb of God, that it descended upon the saints of the church of the Lamb, and upon the covenant people of the Lord, who were scattered upon all the face of the earth; and they were armed with righteousness and with the power of God in great glory." (1 Nephi 14:14.) This is not the end of temple building, for our leaders have prophesied that there will be hundreds of temples dotting the lands of the world where this sacred work will go forth and its influence will be felt. Thus the world will be built and strengthened spiritually, physically, and temporally, all of which is preparatory to the second coming of the Savior.

LOS ANGELES TEMPLE

May all who come within these sacred walls
feel a peaceful, hallowed influence. Cause, O
Lord, that even people who pass the grounds,
or view the temple from afar, may lift their
eyes from the groveling things of sordid life
and look up to thee and thy providence.

◆

From the dedicatory prayer by
David O. McKay
March 11–14, 1956

12

A House of Learning

◆

"One thing I have desired of the Lord, that will I seek after; that I may dwell in the house of the Lord all the days of my life, to behold the beauty of the Lord, and to inquire in his temple." (Psalms 27:4.) King David recognized the temple as a house of learning. In the dedicatory prayer of the Kirtland Temple, Joseph Smith acknowledged the temple to be "a house of prayer, a house of fasting, a house of faith, a house of learning, a house of glory, a house of order, a house of God." (D&C 109:8.)

"Temples are a place of peace and holiness. Let us lay aside the cares and worries of the outside world," President Spencer W. Kimball counseled. "We can then center our minds on the things of the spirit as the great mysteries of life are unfolded to us. Here we learn the answers to those important questions that puzzle all mankind: Where did we come from? Why are we here? Where do we go when this mortal life is finished and over? It would be foolish for us to come to the dedication of a new temple and not have made up our minds that from this hour on we aren't just here for a visit. We are here to receive the word of the Lord." (Seattle Temple Dedication, November 1980.)

"The temple ceremonies are designed by a wise Heavenly Father who has revealed them to us in these last days as a guide and a protection throughout our lives, that you and I might not fail to merit exaltation in the celestial kingdom where God and Christ dwell." (Harold B. Lee, "Enter a Holy Temple," *Improvement Era*, June 1967, p. 144.)

Temples are "a place of instruction for all those who are called to the work of the ministry in all their several callings and offices; that they may be perfected in the understanding of their ministry, in theory, in principle, and in doctrine, in all things pertaining to the kingdom of God on the earth, the keys of which kingdom have been conferred upon you." (D&C 97:13–14.)

If you will go to the temple and remember that the teaching is symbolic you will never go in the proper spirit without coming away with your vision extended, feeling a little more exalted, with your knowledge increased as to things that are spiritual. . . .

The temple ceremony will not be understood at first experience. It will be partly understood. Return again and again and again. Things that have troubled you or things that have been puzzling or things that have been mysterious will become known to you. Many of them will be the quiet, personal things that you really cannot explain to anyone else. But to you they are things known.

In the temple we face the sunlight of truth. The light of the temple, that understanding, shines upon us as does the light of the sun. And the shadows of sin and ignorance and error, of disappointment and failure, fall behind us. . . .

What we gain from the temple will depend to a large degree on what we take to the temple in the way of humility and reverence and a desire to learn. If we are teachable we will be taught by the Spirit, in the temple. . . . Nowhere quite equals the temple. (Boyd K. Packer, *The Holy Temple*, pp. 41–42.)

In the temple we are taught by the Holy Spirit. When we come to the temple properly prepared—that is, with our minds devoid of carnal thoughts and well fed with spiritual food—the Light of Christ comes into focus to enable us to better understand the things of God. The knowledge we gain is not of much value unless it influences our life for good. In the temple, through the power of the Holy Spirit, knowledge is transformed into virtues. A person who attends the temple regularly grows more patient, more long-suffering, and more charitable. He becomes more diligent, more committed, and more dedicated. He develops a greater capacity to love his wife and children and to respect the good qualities and the rights of others. He develops a greater sense of values, becoming more honorable and upright in his dealings and less critical of others. In the temple knowledge is transformed into feelings of the heart, resulting in actions that build character. Thus, the family is strengthened and the community is uplifted to the extent of his influence.

At the conclusion of Joseph Smith's documentation of his amazing vision on the degrees of glory he wrote:

But great and marvelous are the works of the Lord, and the mysteries of his kingdom which he showed unto us, which surpass all understanding in glory, and in might, and in dominion; which he commanded us we should not write while we were yet in the Spirit, and are not lawful for man to utter; neither is man capable to make them known, for they are only to be seen and understood by the power of the Holy Spirit, which God bestows upon those who love him, and purify themselves before him; to whom he grants this privilege of seeing and knowing for themselves; that through the power and manifestation of the Spirit, while in the flesh, they may be able to bear his presence in the world of glory. (D&C 76:114–118.)

"The endowment is so richly symbolic, . . . so packed full of revelations to those who exercise their strength to seek and see, that no human words can explain or make clear the possibilities that reside in the temple service. The endowment which was given by revelation can best be understood by revelation; and to those who seek most vigorously, with pure hearts, will the revelation be greatest." (John A. Widtsoe, "Temple Worship," *Utah Genealogical and Historical Magazine* 12:63.)

The question is often asked, "What book can I read that will explain the endowment?" The answer is simple and short—there isn't one. Perhaps there should not be one. As Elder John A. Widtsoe said, "Only a fool would attempt to describe [the endowment]" ("Temple Worship," *Utah Genealogical and Historical Magazine* 12:63), for man is not capable of explaining the deep spiritual truths represented by the ordinance which constitutes the endowment. As the scripture says, "They are only to be . . . understood by the power of the Holy Spirit." (D&C 76:116.)

May we, as Saints of God, join with King David in his desire to dwell in the house of the Lord and to be taught his marvelous works and the mysteries of the kingdom, which can be communicated by the Holy Spirit only to those pure in heart who are spiritually attuned. Then, for the Saints, the temple becomes a house of learning and a stepping stone to the eternal realms of celestial glory.

NEW ZEALAND TEMPLE

We invoke thy blessing particularly upon the men and women who have so willingly and generously contributed their means, time, and effort to the completion of this imposing and impressive structure. Especially we mention all those who have accepted calls as labor missionaries and literally consecrated their all upon the altar of service. May each contributor be comforted in spirit and prospered many fold. May they be assured that they have the gratitude of thousands, perhaps millions on the other side for whom the prison doors may now be opened and deliverance proclaimed to those who will accept the truth and be set free.

From the dedicatory prayer by
David O. McKay
April 20, 1958

13

The Pathway to Immortality
and Eternal Life

◆

Jesus said, "For behold, this is my work and my glory—to bring to pass the immortality and eternal life of man." (Moses 1:39.) Immortality is the Savior's gift to all mankind. Through his atoning sacrifice he gave to every person who ever was born or ever will be born the guarantee of resurrection from the grave. We learn from the scriptures that "the spirit and the body are the soul of man." (D&C 88:15.) When we die our body goes to the grave and our spirit goes to the world of spirits to await the resurrection.

"Speaking of the resurrection of the dead, concerning those who shall hear the voice of the Son of Man, and [they] shall come forth—they who have done good in the resurrection of the just, and they who have done evil in the resurrection of the unjust." (D&C 76:16–17.) Jesus said, "The hour is coming, and now is, when the dead shall hear the voice of the Son of God: and they that hear shall live . . . and shall come forth; they that have done good, unto the resurrection of life." (John 5:25,29.)

Accordingly, a general resurrection of the righteous spirits took place at the time of the resurrection of the Savior when "the graves were opened; and many bodies of the saints which slept arose, and came out of the graves . . . and went into the holy city, and appeared unto many." (Matthew 27:52-53.) At the same time in ancient America, many of the dead arose from the grave and appeared and ministered unto many of the Saints. (3 Nephi 23:9.) Likewise, there will be a general resurrection of the just when Christ "shall come in the clouds of heaven to reign on the earth over his people. . . . These shall dwell in the presence of God and his Christ forever and ever." (D&C 76:63,62.) The unjust, "they who received not the gospel of Christ, neither the testimony of Jesus, . . . are they who shall not be redeemed . . . until the last resurrection, until the

Lord . . . shall have finished his work." (D&C 76:82,85.) Resurrection brings immortality, which is to live forever in the resurrected state with body and spirit inseparably connected.

Eternal life is the kind of life our Heavenly Father lives. It is "the greatest of all the gifts of God" (D&C 14:7) but must be earned by obedience to the laws and ordinances of the gospel. The laws of the gospel are found in the scriptures. "Baptism for the dead, an ordinance opening the door to the celestial kingdom to worthy persons not privileged to undergo gospel schooling while in mortality, is a temple ordinance, an ordinance of salvation. All other temple ordinances—washings, anointings, endowments, sealings—pertain to exaltation within the celestial kingdom. Celestial marriage is the gate which puts men on the path leading to the highest of three heavens within the celestial world. (D&C 131:1–4.) All of these ordinances of exaltation are performed in the temples for both the living and the dead." (Bruce R. McConkie, *Mormon Doctrine*, p. 779.) Without receiving his temple ordinances, no person, worlds without end, can attain eternal life or exaltation. There is no other way.

Some members believe that because they have been baptized and have received their temple blessings they will receive eternal life without further effort on their part. Some consider the gospel as a smorgasbord from which they can select concepts that conform to their own philosophies and discard those that do not. However, that this is not the Lord's plan is quite obvious to any who study the scriptures, listen to modern prophets, and attend to their temple duties honestly and regularly.

The oath and covenant of the Melchizedek Priesthood found in D&C 84:33–41 briefly describes what we must do to earn eternal life and the benefits therefrom: we must demonstrate faithfulness "unto the obtaining of these two priesthoods . . . and the magnifying [our] calling." "Therefore all that my Father hath shall be given unto him"—this verse describes the reward. These blessings require the priesthood and faithfulness in building the kingdom of God. Although the oath and covenant is received by the worthy male member of the Melchizedek Priesthood, the woman is essential to the promised blessings. The Apostle Paul declared: "Neither is the man without the woman, neither the woman without the man, in the Lord." (1 Corinthians 11:11.) The Lord has explained that "in the celestial glory there are three heavens or degrees; and in order to obtain the highest, a man must enter into this order of the priest-hood (meaning the new and everlasting covenant of marriage); and if he does not, he cannot obtain it. He may enter into the other, but that is the end of his kingdom; he cannot have an increase." (D&C 131:1–4.) The covenant of eternal marriage binds one to the other so as to share opportunities, responsibilities, and rewards. This does not require one to be a bishop or a stake president or a Relief Society president to gain eternal life, but to serve diligently and strive to fulfill whatever assignments or responsibilities one receives.

We are charged to "call upon the Lord, that his kingdom may go forth upon the earth, that the inhabitants thereof may receive it, and be prepared for the days to come, in the which the Son of Man shall come down in heaven, clothed in the brightness of his glory, to meet the kingdom of God which is set up on the earth. Where-fore, may the kingdom of God go forth, that the kingdom of heaven may come, that thou, O God, mayest be glorified in heaven so on earth." (D&C 65:5–6.)

Speaking to Church members in the early days of the Restora-tion and to us today as well, the Lord placed the cloak of responsibilty on our shoulders when he said, "The kingdom is yours." (D&C 62:9.) And thus we have the assignment individu-ally and collectively to prepare the world for the second coming of the Savior. While doing so, we have the opportunity of earning exaltation in the celestial kingdom of God by magnifying our indi-vidual callings and enduring faithfully to the end.

LONDON TEMPLE

With humility and deep gratitude we acknowledge thy nearness, thy divine guidance and inspiration. Help us, we pray thee, to become even more susceptible in our spiritual response to thee.

Temples are built to thy holy name as a means of uniting thy people, living and dead, in bonds of faith, of peace and of love throughout eternity.

◆

From the dedicatory prayer by
David O. McKay
September 7–9, 1958

14

Opening the Door to Celestial Glory

◆

"God is no respecter of persons." (Acts 10:34.) He will not give privileges concerning eternal destiny to one generation and withhold them from another, to the people of one nation and not another, nor to one race and not another, for "he inviteth them all to come unto him and partake of his goodness; and he denieth none that come unto him, black and white, bond and free, male and female; and he remembereth the heathen; and all are alike unto God, both Jew and Gentile." (2 Nephi 26:33.)

The prophet Alma became so enthusiastic about missionary service that he exclaimed, "O that I were an angel, and could have the wish of mine heart, that I might go forth and speak with the trump of God, with a voice to shake the earth, and cry repentance unto every people!" (Alma 29:1.) But after reasoning with himself and upon further consideration, he said: "Now, seeing that I know these things, . . . why should I desire that I were an angel, that I could speak unto all the ends of the earth? For behold, the Lord doth grant unto all nations, of their own nation and tongue, to teach his word, yea, in wisdom, all that he seeth fit that they should have; therefore we see that the Lord doth counsel in wisdom, according to that which is just and true." (Alma 29:6–8.)

Wilford Woodruff said, "The generations that have passed and gone without hearing the gospel of Christ; and the generations that have passed and gone without hearing the gospel in its fullness, power and glory will never be held responsible by God for not obeying it, neither will he bring them under condemnation for rejecting a law they never saw or understood; and if they live up to the light they had they are justified so far, and they have to be preached to in the spirit world." (JD 18:190–91.)

Speaking to this point of eternal justice the Prophet Joseph Smith said: "One dies and is buried, having never heard the gospel of reconciliation; to the other the message is sent; he hears and embraces it, and is made the heir of eternal life. Shall the one become the partaker of glory and the other be consigned to hopeless perdition? Is there no chance for his escape? Sectarianism answers 'none.' Such an idea is worse than atheism." (*HC* 4:425–26.)

"For for this cause was the gospel preached also to them that are dead, that they might be judged according to men in the flesh, but live according to God in the spirit," wrote the Apostle Peter. (1 Peter 4:6.) Of the redemption of the dead, President Joseph F. Smith said: "We have a mission to perform for and in their behalf; we have a certain work to do in order to liberate those who, because of the ignorance and the unfavorable circumstances in which they were placed while here, are unprepared for eternal life; we have to open the door for them, by performing ordinances which they cannot perform for themselves and which are essential to their release from the 'prison house' to come forth and live according to God in the spirit and be judged according to men in the flesh." (*JD* 19:264.)

Between the time of the Savior's crucifixion and his resurrection, "he went and preached unto the spirits in prison." (1 Peter 3:19.)

> And there were gathered together in one place an innumerable company of the spirits of the just, who had been faithful in the testimony of Jesus while they lived in mortality. . . . While this vast multitude waited and conversed . . . the Son of God appeared, declaring liberty to the captives who had been faithful; and there he preached to them the everlasting gospel, the doctrine of the resurrection and the redemption of mankind from the fall, and from individual sins on conditions of repentance. But unto the wicked he did not go. . . . But behold, from among the righteous, he organized his forces . . . and commissioned them to go forth and carry the light of the gospel to them that were in darkness, even to all the spirits of men; and thus was the gospel preached to the dead. . . . The dead who repent will be redeemed, through obedience to the ordinances of the house of God, and after they have paid the penalty of their transgressions, and are washed clean, shall receive a reward according to their works, for they are heirs of salvation. (D&C 138:12, 18–20, 30, 58–59.)

Baptism is essential for entrance into the celestial kingdom. So we are baptized for the dead. We also receive other saving ordinances vicariously for the dead. The dead cannot perform these ordinances for themselves, for they are earthly ordinances only to be performed in the house of the Lord. All temple ordinances, except baptism for the dead, pertain to exaltation in the celestial kingdom and not merely to admission to that world. When the prophet first administered the endowment in this dispensation, he said it embraced "all those plans and principles by which anyone is enabled to secure the fullness of those blessings which have been prepared for the Church of the Firstborn." (*Teachings of the Prophet Joseph Smith*, p. 237.)

Many people in Christendom believe that man can gain salvation by grace alone and that salvation means to be united with God. We believe that all men gain immortality, which is a free gift from God as a result of the atoning sacrifice, and that immortality is the reuniting of the body and the spirit in resurrection. We are taught by latter-day revelation that salvation in the celestial kingdom of God is salvation by grace coupled with obedience to the laws and ordinances of the gospel. Faith, repentance, baptism, and receipt of the Holy Ghost are necessary, together with continual striving for righteousness to the end of one's mortal probation. Baptism opens the door into the celestial kingdom. Other temple ordinances open another door into exaltation in the celestial kingdom. This is the quest of the true Saints of God: to learn, understand, and live so as to receive the exaltation which can only be received as we open doors for ourselves and for our dead—for "they without us cannot be made perfect—neither can we without our dead be made perfect." (D&C 128:15.)

OAKLAND TEMPLE

This temple . . . is a monument testifying to
the faith and loyalty of the members of thy
Church in the payment of their tithes and offerings. We thank thee for every effort that has
been put forth by the members, from every
sacrifice that has been made by the young boys
and girls who have given of their dimes and
dollars, the millionaire who gave of his thousands.

◆

From the dedicatory prayer by
David O. McKay
November 17–19, 1964

15

Priesthood Authority

◆

In September of 1823, the angel Moroni appeared to Joseph Smith in the upper bedroom of his father's home in Manchester, New York. In relaying his message he quoted Malachi 4:5–6 from the Old Testament with certain changes: "Behold, I will reveal unto you the Priesthood, by the hand of Elijah the prophet, before the coming of the great and dreadful day of the Lord. And he shall plant in the hearts of the children the promises made to the fathers, and the hearts of the children shall turn to their fathers. If it were not so, the whole earth would be utterly wasted at his coming." (D&C 2.) When Elijah appeared to Joseph Smith and Oliver Cowdery in the Kirtland Temple on April 3, 1836, he announced that the time had fully come for the fulfillment of Malachi's prophecy. (D&C 110:14–15.)

From whom did Joseph Smith and Oliver Cowdery receive the priesthood? They received the Aaronic Priesthood under the hands of John the Baptist in May of 1829. They received the Melchizedek Priesthood under the hands of Peter, James, and John in June of 1829. Then what did the Lord mean when he said he would reveal the priesthood by the hand of Elijah the prophet? "Elijah was the last [Old Testament] Prophet that held the keys of the Priesthood. . . . He holds the keys of the authority to administer in all the ordinances of the Priesthood; and without the authority is given, the ordinances could not be administered in righteousness." (Joseph Smith, *HC* 4:211.)

It was Elijah who bestowed the keys of sealing power upon Peter, James, and John on the Mount of Transfiguration during the ministry of the Savior. (See Matthew 16:18–19; 17:1–9.) It was also Elijah who bestowed the keys of the sealing power upon Joseph Smith and Oliver Cowdery in the Kirtland Temple on April 3, 1836. (See D&C 110:12–16.) The keys of the sealing power consist of the power to bind or to seal in heaven that which is bound or sealed on earth and encompasses the authority to administer the ordinances of the Melchizedek Priesthood.

"And this greater priesthood administereth the gospel and holdeth the key of the mysteries of the kingdom, even the key of the knowledge of God. Therefore, in the ordinances thereof, the power of godliness is manifest. And without the ordinances thereof, and the authority of the priesthood, the power of godliness is not manifest unto men in the flesh." (D&C 84:19–21.)

In one sense, the mysteries of the kingdom mentioned above are those principles of the gospel we do not understand. When we come to understand them, they are no longer mysteries. But in a deeper sense, the "mysteries" are the temple ordinances, which are symbolic of profound spiritual truths only to be understood by the Spirit. They have been referred to since antiquity as the mysteries of the kingdom. (See *Pistis Sophia*, trans. Carl Schmidt [Copenhagen: Nordisk Forlag, 1925], as quoted in Hugh Nibley, "Appendix 4: From the Pistis Sophis," *The Message of the Joseph Smith Papyri* [Salt Lake City: Deseret Book Company, 1975], p. 274.)

It is the author's opinion that the key to the knowledge of God is the sacred endowment received in the house of the Lord, for if one who has received the temple endowment will remain faithful to the covenants made in the temple, study the scriptures, and return to the temple regularly for temple worship, his mind will be enlightened and his understanding quickened relative to eternal truths of God. As the dew distills upon the earth from heaven above, so an understanding of the truths of the gospel will distill into his mind. He will be taught by the Holy Spirit. He must study, however, for the Holy Ghost will not inspire him if his mind is not spiritually prepared. Thus the endowment is a key to knowledge of God.

The power of godliness is manifest only when the authority of the priesthood is exercised in connection with the ordinances of the Melchizedek Priesthood, as in the sacred temple ordinances, blessings, bestowal of the Holy Ghost, and ordinations, for example. In 1841 the Lord instructed the Saints: "But I command you, . . . to build a house unto me; . . . for therein are the keys of the holy priesthood ordained [set in order], that you may receive honor and glory." (D&C 124:31, 34.) Thus the Lord succinctly expressed the purpose for building temples, for knowledge, obedience, and sacrifice—about which we learn in the temple—are the pathway to honor and glory.

President John Taylor said: "When Elijah the prophet appeared to Joseph Smith he committed to him the keys of this dispensation; and hence we are at work building Temples; but some of us hardly know why. . . . There are ordinances associated behind these things that go back into eternity; and forward into eternity; that are the offspring of God, that are intended for the welfare, the happiness and the exaltation of mankind; for those who are living and those that are dead and for those that will live hereafter, pertaining both to our progenitors and our posterity. And that is one of those keys that have been turned." (*JD* 21:95.)

Recall in part the words of Moroni to Joseph Smith: "And he shall plant in the hearts of the children the promises made to *the* fathers and the hearts of the children shall turn to *their* fathers." (D&C 2:2.) Elder Joseph Fielding Smith explained that "this expression has reference to certain promises made to those who died without a knowledge of the gospel, and without the opportunity of receiving the sealing ordinances of the Priesthood in matters pertaining to their exaltation. According to these promises, the children in the latter days are to perform all such ordinances in behalf of the dead." ("The Promises Made to the Fathers," *Improvement Era*, July 1922, p. 829.)

It is interesting to note that Moroni in the first instance refers to "the" fathers and in the second to "their" fathers. Why didn't he use the word *their* in both instances? Could the scripture have additional meaning that *the* fathers are Abraham, Isaac, and Jacob and that the promises referred to might include the Abrahamic Covenant which was given by the Lord to each of those three individually and separately? The Abrahamic Covenant promises that our dispensation will bear "this ministry and Priesthood unto all nations" and "the blessings of the Gospel, which are the blessings of salvation, even of life eternal." (Abraham 2:9–11.)

Today we have many thousands of missionaries taking this ministry and priesthood to the world. We have or soon will have temples—in lands where Church membership is sufficient to justify a temple—where the ordinances necessary for salvation and eternal life are available to members in their own lands.

President Spencer W. Kimball said, "I hope to see us dissolve the artificial boundary line we so often place between missionary work and temple and genealogical work, because it is the same great redemptive work!" ("The Things of Eternity—Stand We in Jeopardy?" *Ensign*, January 1977, p. 3.) Both are necessary "to bring to pass the immortality and eternal life of man" (Abraham 1:39) "else the whole earth would be utterly wasted at his coming." (D&C 2:3.)

OGDEN TEMPLE

It has been our privilege, as guided by the whisperings of the Spirit, to build unto thee this temple, which we now present unto thee as another of thy holy houses. We humbly pray that thou wilt accept this edifice and pour out thy blessings upon it as a house to which thou wilt come and in which thy Spirit will direct all that is done, that it may be accepted unto thee.

◆

From the dedicatory prayer by
Joseph Fielding Smith
January 18–20, 1972

16

The Holy Ghost, the Priesthood, and Temples

◆

The Prophet Joseph Smith was once asked by the president of the United States how we differed in our religion from other religions of the day. He said we differ in the mode of baptism and the gift of the Holy Ghost by the laying on of hands. (See *HC* 4:42.) From the Doctrine and Covenants we learn that "the Father has a body of flesh and bones as tangible as man's; the Son also; but the Holy Ghost has not a body of flesh and bones, but is a personage of Spirit. Were it not so, the Holy Ghost could not dwell in us." (D&C 130:22.) The Apostle Paul, speaking to the Saints of his day, said, "Know ye not that ye are the temple of God, and that the [Holy Ghost] dwelleth in you?" (1 Corinthians 3:16; also see 1 Corinthians 6:19.) The mission of the Holy Ghost is to bear witness in the hearts of men that Jesus is the Christ. The Holy Ghost is given to a person through the authority of the Melchizedek Priesthood. Having received this sacred blessing, he may enjoy the constant companionship of the Holy Ghost so long as he remains worthy. In the Book of Mormon, Moroni said, "And by the power of the Holy Ghost ye may know the truth of all things" (Moroni 10:5.); thus, the Holy Ghost is a communicator of truth from God to man. Learning how to receive communications from God through the Holy Ghost is important to our eternal destiny.

Following the crucifixion of the Savior, "when the doors were shut where the disciples were assembled . . . he shewed unto them [the wounds in] his hands and his side . . . and saith unto them, Receive ye the Holy Ghost." (John 20:19–22.) Since the beginning of time, the authority to bestow the Holy Ghost has been delegated to those to whom the Melchizedek Priesthood has been given. The Prophet Joseph Smith and Oliver Cowdery were given the Melchizedek Priesthood by Peter, James, and John through a personal visitation. They in turn had received it from the Savior. This is an important part of the restitution of all things spoken of by the Apostle Peter as recorded in Acts 3:19–21. And thus the blessings and ordinances of the Holy Priesthood are available to us today as they were in the days of the Savior's ministry, including the power to bestow the Holy Ghost.

One holding the Melchizedek Priesthood has the authority to perform other sacred ordinances as well, such as health blessings, ordinations within the priesthood, patriarchal blessings (when ordained to do so), specific ordinances performed in the temple (when set apart to do so), and sealing families (when given the sealing power). Peter received the keys of the sealing power, as promised by the Savior (Matthew 16:19) on the Mount of Transfiguration. Joseph Smith and Oliver Cowdery were given the keys of the sealing power by Elijah the prophet on April 3, 1836, in the Kirtland Temple as related in the 110th section of the Doctrine and Covenants. These keys have been relayed to successive prophets down to our present-day prophet. This authority to seal has been given to selected qualified Melchizedek Priesthood holders in this day who perform these ordinances in the temples of the Lord.

Elder Boyd K. Packer related the following experience concerning President Spencer W. Kimball, who at the time was the Lord's living prophet:

> In 1976 an area general conference was held in Copenhagen, Denmark. Following the closing session, President Kimball expressed a desire to visit the Vor Frue Church, where the Thorvaldsen statues of the Christus and of the Twelve Apostles stand. . . .
>
> Arrangements were quickly made for us to be admitted. . . .
>
> To the front of the church, behind the altar, stands the familiar statue of the Christus with his arms turned forward and somewhat outstretched, the hands showing the imprint of the nails, the wound in his side clearly visible. Along each side stand the statues of the Apostles, Peter at the front on the right side of the church. . . .
>
> In his hand, depicted in marble, is a set of heavy keys. President Kimball pointed to them and explained what they symbolized. Then . . . he turned to [the mission president] and with unaccustomed sternness pointed his finger at him and said with firm, impressive words, "I want you to tell every Lutheran in Denmark that they do not hold the keys! I hold the keys! We hold the real keys and we use them every day." (*The Holy Temple*, p. 83.)

Yes, the keys of the sealing power are used every day in the temples of the Lord to unite families. Wife is sealed to husband and children to parents for time and eternity. When a marriage is solemnized in the temple for time and eternity, an eternal family is formed. Promises are given in the temple regarding the future of the family, predicated upon the faithfulness of each family member. Instructions are also given as to how one can bring those promises to reality.

Faithful Latter-day Saints begin their eternal family here and can enjoy here much of that peace, joy, and love that will characterize family relations in the celestial kingdom of God. Regular visits to the temple give one a greater resolve and commitment to the family and a better understanding of the expanded family unit. Also, the spirit in the temple is transmitted to the home, which brings greater peace and harmony to the family. Without the Melchizedek Priesthood, neither the support and guidance of the Holy Ghost in our lives (which is so precious to us in our homes and daily affairs), nor the blessings of a forever family in the celestial kingdom of God will be ours.

In answer to the inquirer's question, Joseph Smith, in addition to the answer he gave concerning the Holy Ghost, might well have said, "We have the priesthood of God," or "We have the blessings of the temple," all three of which are closely allied.

PROVO TEMPLE

We dedicate this temple to thee, the Lord. We
dedicate it as a house of baptism, a house of
endowment, a house of marriage, a house of
righteousness for the living and the dead.

We dedicate the font and ordinance rooms and
especially the sealing rooms, that they may be
kept holy and that thy protecting care may be
over them, and that thy Spirit may ever be
present to enlighten those who attend.

———————————◆———————————

From the dedicatory prayer by
Joseph Fielding Smith
February 9, 1972

17

Symbolism and Temple Ordinances

◆

We live in a world of symbols. We make a vertical mark with a pencil and it represents *one*. We put a small circle to the right of it and it represents *ten*. To the left we put an *S* with a vertical line through it and it now represents ten dollars. We add some more small circles to the right and it represents necessities and luxuries that we can purchase: a new home, a new car, or freedom from financial anxieties. We add some more zeroes to the right and it represents status, influence, power, and wealth. Symbols are a part of our way of living.

Teaching in the temple is symbolic. From an article by Elder John A. Widtsoe, a renowned scientist, educator, and member of the Quorum of the Twelve Apostles, we learn the following:

> No man or woman can come out of the temple endowed as he should be, unless he has seen, beyond the symbol, the mighty realities for which the symbols stand. . . . The endowment itself . . . is a series of symbols of vast realities, too vast for full understanding. . . . The endowment is so richly symbolic that only a fool would attempt to describe it; it is so packed full of revelations to those who exercise their strength to seek and see, that no human words can explain or make clear the possibilities that reside in the temple service. The endowment which was given by revelation can best be understood by revelation; and to those who seek most vigorously, with pure hearts, will the revelation be the greatest. (*Utah Genealogical and Historical Magazine* 12:61–63.)

When President David O. McKay was ninety-one years of age, he addressed the General Authorities in the Salt Lake Temple just prior to a general conference. He spoke at length about the temple ordinances and the temple ceremonies. Elder Boyd K. Packer recalled the occasion: ''I remember that his big hands were in front of him with his fingers interlocked. He stood gazing as people sometimes do when pondering a deep question. Then he spoke: 'Brethren, I think I am finally beginning to understand.' " (*The Holy Temple*, p. 263.)

President McKay had served as a member of the Quorum of the Twelve for approximately fifty years and as President of the Church for twenty years. I think I understand what he meant when he said, "I think I am beginning to understand." The temple endowment has such great depth that the more a person learns about the endowment, the more he realizes that there is much more to learn than he had suspected. Thus, regardless of his background and experience and depth of study, he always feels that he is just beginning to understand the endowment.

Elder H. Burke Peterson expressed this well when, after serving for a year as President of the Jordan River Temple, he said, "It is my impression that man does not have the capacity to explain the endowment to another man. I think that is good. I don't think he is supposed to. I think there are many who try, and I believe that is unfortunate because I think we must be careful in trying to explain some elements of the endowment that have not been explained." Then he went on to tell about his feelings and understandings: "I have had feelings I have never had before. I have had resolves come to me when I needed to have resolves come to me. There are things I hadn't felt that I didn't know I hadn't felt. There are things I understand that I didn't know I didn't understand. I don't believe that man can explain the endowment adequately. We can talk about the process, but it is a power. The endowment is a power, and it can come to us only by revelation. We must feel the endowment to know its meaning." ("The Temple and Its Influence in Perfecting the Members of the Church," First Quorum of the Seventy Meeting Address, 20 February 1986.)

It would be unfortunate if the temple endowment were so shallow that we understood it in one brief session. When we properly prepare ourselves and strive to understand, we learn more about the meaning of the endowment each time we come to the temple. In our search for understanding, each visit becomes a special experience and our minds become further enlightened. Temple work is not *work* but an educational experience that one finds difficult to describe. Joseph Smith wrote of the great and marvelous works and the mysteries of the kingdom that the Lord showed him and Sidney Rigdon "which surpass all understanding . . . in might, and in dominion." He explained that man is not "capable to make them known, for they are only to be seen and understood by the power of the Holy Spirit, which God bestows on those who love him, and purify themselves before him.'' (D&C 76:114,116.)

And so it is with those who avail themselves regularly of the blessings of the temple: words cannot express the feelings, the joy, and the satisfaction that come into their hearts and minds. As they remain faithful and study the scriptures, their vision is expanded; they grow up in the Lord and gradually receive a fulness of the Holy Ghost. (D&C 109:14–15.)

How fortunate we are to have access to a house of God where we can partake of the fulness of the gospel of Jesus Christ and be taught from on high!

WASHINGTON TEMPLE

We are so grateful, our Father, that thy Son has thrown wide open the doors of the prisons for the multitudes who are waiting in the spirit world.

Wilt thou deign to make this temple thy house and let holy angels visit it to deliver thy messages, as the rushing of mighty winds with power and glory.

◆

From the dedicatory prayer by
Spencer W. Kimball
November 19–22, 1974

18

To Know God Is Eternal Life

◆

In this life of strife and uncertainty, we obtain comfort and peace as we strive to live lives of obedience to the principles of the gospel. This comfort comes from the Lord in answer to his promise, "Draw near unto me and I will draw near unto you." (D&C 88:63.)

When Oliver Cowdery was assisting Joseph Smith in translating the Book of Mormon, he asked the Lord for a witness to assure him of the authenticity of the work. The Lord responded. Shortly thereafter, Oliver Cowdery, wanting reassurance, asked again. Through the Prophet Joseph the Lord answered: "Verily, verily, I say unto you, if you desire a further witness, cast your mind upon the night that you cried unto me in your heart, that you might know concerning the truth of these things. Did I not speak peace to your mind concerning the matter? What greater witness can you have than from God?" (D&C 6:22–23.)

As we seek this inner peace let us consider the words of the Lord given to us through the Prophet Joseph Smith: "And inasmuch as my people build a house unto me in the name of the Lord, and do not suffer any unclean thing to come into it, that it be not defiled, my glory shall rest upon it [the Holy Spirit abides in the temple]; yea, and my presence shall be there, for I will come into it [when the Lord comes to earth, where would he come except to one of his temples?], and all the pure in heart that shall come into it shall *see* God." (D&C 97:15–16, italics added.)

President Spencer W. Kimball spoke in my home ward sacrament meeting one Sunday and said that there are people in this world who are pure in heart. Then he made reference to a little old lady who lived in the corner house down the street, and I understood what he meant. There are people among us who are pure in heart. The Lord is not talking about someone who, in the realm of possibility, might be pure in heart. I believe there are many people who are pure in heart. I believe the Lord means what he says when he states that *all* the pure in heart that shall come into the temple shall see God.

Elder Bruce R. McConkie, in his book *A New Witness for the Articles of Faith*, wrote a chapter on personal revelation in which he discussed the reality of seeing God in this life with our mortal eyes. "There is a true doctrine," he wrote, "that mortal man, while in the flesh, has it in his power to see the Lord, to stand in his presence, to feel the nail marks in his hands and feet, and to receive from him such blessings as are reserved for those only who keep all his commandments and who are qualified for that eternal life which includes being in his presence forever. . . . We must not wrest the scriptures and suppose that the promises of seeing the Lord refer to some future day, either a Millennial or a celestial day, days in which, as we all know, the Lord will be present. The promises apply to this mortal sphere in which we now live." (Pp. 492, 495.)

We should seek his face, living our lives in such a way that we might be worthy to receive such a marvelous manifestation. There are many righteous men who have received such a manifestation although there are many righteous men who have not. But the Lord said, "*All* the pure in heart that shall come into [the temple] shall see God." (D&C 97:16, italics added.) I believe that many members of the Church who come to the temple are pure in heart. Have they *all* seen God with their natural eyes? I would venture to say, "No."

In the English language the word *see* is used in many different ways, each of which is supported by a definition found in Webster's Dictionary. For example, "Will you see my daughter home?" means to escort her home. "I'll see about that" means to investigate a matter. "I'm going to see my mother" means to visit her. "Don't you see what I mean?" means to understand. Webster's Dictionary gives twenty-two different definitions for the word *see*, one of which is "to perceive by the eye." Should the Lord be confined to just one definition, when we ourselves use the word in so many different ways?

Webster gives these definitions: to come to know—*to discover*; to form a mental picture of—*to visualize*; to be aware of—*to recognize*; to perceive the meaning or importance of—*to understand*.

Let us place these definitions into the context of the scripture: "And all the pure in heart that shall come into [the temple] shall"—

–come to know God.

–discover God.

–be able to visualize God.

–become aware of God.

–recognize God.

–perceive the importance of God.

–come to understand God.

When Nephi and his two brothers returned from Jerusalem with the plates of Laban, their father, Lehi, announced to them, "Behold, I have dreamed a dream; or, in other words, I have seen a vision." (1 Nephi 8:2.) Not only can we see with our eyes but we can also see with our minds, in vision that can be more powerful, more enduring, and more meaningful than that limited to the gift of eyesight.

According to Webster's definitions, one can see God by perceiving with the eye, one can see him by coming to know him, one can see him by discovering him, one can see him by visualizing him, one can see him by becoming aware of him, one can see him by recognizing him and his works, one can see him by perceiving his importance, and one can see him by coming to understand him.

The Savior said, "And this is life eternal, that they might know thee the only true God, and Jesus Christ, whom thou hast sent." (John 17:3.) If we are to attain eternal life, we must come to know God. We can know him by better understanding him. We can better understand him by coming to the temple regularly, where our minds will be enlightened, our understanding quickened, our lives enriched, and where we will be at peace with the world. Therefore, in a very literal way the temple becomes a stepping-stone to eternal life, where we cannot only see God, but we can also be with him face to face through his grace in this life and through our obedience in the eternities to come.

SAO PAULO TEMPLE

Our Father, may peace abide in all the homes of thy Saints. May holy angels guard them. May prosperity shine upon them and sickness and disease be rebuked from their midst. May their land be made fruitful. May the waters be pure and the climate tempered to the comfort and well-being of thy people.

Bless the poor of thy people, that the cry of want and suffering may not ascend unto thy Saints.

◆

From the dedicatory prayer by
Spencer W. Kimball
October 30, 1978

19

Learning the Lord's Way

◆

President David O. McKay often used the word *inculcate*. In his talks he counseled parents to inculcate into their children the principles of the gospel. Webster's Dictionary defines *inculcate* as "to teach and impress by frequent repetitions or admonitions."

This is the method the Lord uses in teaching the members of the Church through the scriptures and the temple. Members come to the temple first to receive their own endowments and then return to act as proxies for their progenitors and others who have not had the opportunity of receiving temple blessings for themselves. Thus a faithful individual is exposed to the message of the temple ordinances over and over again.

The words of the ordinances were given us from the Lord. They are sacred and meaningful and should be held in reverence. "For my thoughts are not your thoughts, neither are your ways my ways, saith the Lord. For as the heavens are higher than the earth, so are my ways higher than your ways, and my thoughts than your thoughts." (Isaiah 55:8–9.)

It would be unfortunate if the temple endowment were so elementary that it could be understood in one exposure. Quite to the contrary—the ordinances of the temple are symbolic and have profound spiritual significance. Having received the endowment, if a person will remain faithful to his temple covenants, study the scriptures, ask the Lord for understanding, and return to the temple regularly to act as proxy for his kindred dead—as he contemplates the meaning of the ordinances and symbols—his mind will be enlightened so as to come to an increased understanding of the endowment. The spiritual truths therein are of such magnitude that perhaps no one in this life will understand their full significance.

To get the most out of temple service, a person should prepare himself through prayer and study and by eliminating carnal thoughts from his mind, for nothing unclean can enter the presence of the Lord.

The bodies of those who have had the Holy Ghost bestowed upon them are temples of God, and the Holy Spirit dwells within them. When they defile their bodies by unclean thoughts, the Holy Spirit leaves, their bodies are no longer temples of God, and they lose the benefit of companionship with God. Thoughts of the natural mind can be controlled by eliminating jealousies and fears and humbling ourselves before the Lord. We can fill our minds with spiritual thoughts by reading the scriptures daily. We are taught in and out of the temple by the Holy Spirit when our mind is properly attuned. The Holy Ghost does not work on a mind that is devoid of spiritual thoughts.

We say, "The temple is beautiful!" And it is. The architecture is beautiful, the grounds are beautiful, but that is only external beauty. That which is most beautiful in the temple is the spirit that prevails. This spirit is enhanced by the fact that the temple is a house of learning where one, through the Spirit of the Lord, comes to a greater understanding of the significance and meaning of the temple ordinances, the plan of salvation, and other wonderful gospel truths. Indeed, the temple is a beautiful, wonderful place of learning.

When a person visits the temple, he should periodically serve in the washing, anointing, and clothing area, where he can hear the great promises made by the Lord to those who are faithful. Also, he should serve occasionally with a sealing group where wives are sealed to husbands and children to parents for time and eternity. Again he hears the words of the promises made to him, which become inculcated into the heart, mind, and soul of each person who is so involved.

In the endowment session, too, a person attending the temple is repeatedly exposed to the words of the covenants and ordinances. The more we hear these words and study their meaning, the more beautiful they become. We are taught sacred truths by frequent repetition that build and magnify those who strive to improve. The words of the endowment are not unlike the scriptures. The better we understand the scriptures, the more qualified we become to understand those things in the scriptures that we do not understand. Likewise, the better we understand the endowment, the more qualified we become to understand those things about the endowment we do not understand, for the Lord gives us line upon line, precept upon precept, here a little and there a little until the perfect day.

TOKYO TEMPLE

Kind Father, bless all those who come to this temple, that they may do so with humble hearts, in cleanliness and honor and integrity. We are grateful for these Saints, for their devotion and their faith, for their worthiness and their determination to be pure and holy.

We are jubilant this day, our Holy Father, and have hearts filled with praise to thee that thou hast permitted us to see the completion of this temple and to see this day for which we have so long hoped and toiled and prayed.

◆

From the dedicatory prayer by
Spencer W. Kimball
October 27–29, 1980

20

From Material Imperfection
to Spiritual Perfection

◆

King Benjamin in his old age invited his people to come to the temple to hear his farewell address. Because so many came, he was unable to accommodate them in the temple. He had a tower constructed from which he spoke: "My brethren, all ye that have assembled yourselves together, you that can hear my words which I shall speak unto you this day; for I have not commanded you to come up hither to trifle with the words which I shall speak, but that you should hearken unto me, and open your ears that ye may hear, and your hearts that ye may understand, and your minds that the mysteries of God may be unfolded to your view." (Mosiah 2:9.)

King Benjamin's words were appropriate as a greeting to his people whom he had invited to the temple, for a temple is a place of learning—a place of instruction concerning eternal truths. The Prophet Joseph Smith made reference to this in his dedicatory prayer of the Kirtland Temple. He addressed Heavenly Father and said, "And do thou grant, Holy Father, that all those who shall worship in this house may be taught words of wisdom, . . . that they may seek learning even by study, and also by faith, . . . that they may grow up in thee, and receive a fulness of the Holy Ghost." (D&C 109:14–15.) To grow up in the Lord means to mature in gospel understanding. To receive a fulness of the Holy Ghost is to receive a fulness of knowledge, for the Holy Ghost is a communicator from God to man. He reveals truth and knowledge to God's children.

Father Abraham made some interesting statements concerning the gaining of knowledge that might well have been related to temple work. Let us remember that Abraham paid tithing to Melchizedek, and also received the priesthood under his hands. (Alma 13:15, D&C 84:14.) The renowned historian Josephus recorded that Melchizedek, who was the king of Salem, built a temple in Salem and changed the name of the city from Salem to Jerusalem. (Josephus, *Complete Works*, p. 588.) If we can accept this information from Josephus as correct, then Abraham probably had access to a temple of the Lord. Abraham wrote:

"I sought for the blessings of the fathers,"

[in the light of what follows might Abraham have been referring to his temple blessings?]

"and the right whereunto I should be ordained to administer the same;"

[could he have been desiring the right to administer the ordinances of the Melchizedek Priesthood performed in the temple of the Lord?]

"having been myself a follower of righteousness, desiring also to be one who possessed great knowledge, and to be a greater follower of righteousness, and to possess a greater knowledge,"

[knowing that in the temple he could gain greater knowledge concerning things of God, might Abraham have been desiring to receive the sacred endowment?]

"and to be a father of many nations, a prince of peace, and desiring to receive instructions, and to keep the commandments of God,"

[these desires are consistent with temple blessings and covenants]

"I became a rightful heir, a High Priest, holding the right belonging to the fathers. . . . I sought for mine appointment unto the Priesthood according to the appointment of God unto the fathers concerning the seed." (Abraham 1:2, 4.)

Does this not perhaps suggest that Abraham knew the role of the priesthood and its relationship to the temple? The Book of Abraham facsimile number 2 and the explanation of figures 3 and 7 found on the page facing the facsimile provide evidence of Abraham's knowledge of temple ordinances. It is likely that he wrote the book of Abraham after he sought for and received his appointment unto the priesthood and at a time when his understanding of these matters had matured. This would reflect a deeper spiritual maturity than it would have had it been written at the time he was ordained a high priest.

There is much to learn about the truths of eternity, for "the glory of God is intelligence, or, in other words, light and truth." (D&C 93:36.) "Whatever principle of intelligence we attain unto in this life, it will rise with us in the resurrection. And if a person gains more knowledge and intelligence in this life through his diligence and obedience than another, he will have so much the advantage in the world to come." (D&C 130:18–19.) "It is impossible for a man to be saved in ignorance." (D&C 131:6.) Much can be learned in the temple of the Lord. Every time we come to the temple we should strive to understand the spiritual truths of which the ordinances are symbolic.

Elder John A. Widtsoe wrote:

> Those who enter the temples and desire to obtain the most from the experience must seek to purify their hearts in preparation. Only those who do so share fully in the blessings that flow from the temple. Unworthy persons, or those with minds fixed upon external things, who may enter, will not sense the essential beauty and value of the temple ordinances. The pure in heart shall know that God is in His temple. It must always be kept in mind that the work in the temples, as in all divisions of the Church, is done by mortal, imperfect men, but that the story and lessons and issues of the temple endowment are divine and perfect. All who enter into the temple must look through material imperfection into spiritual perfection. ("The House of the Lord," *Improvement Era*, April 1936, p. 228.)

The Prophet Joseph Smith said: "When you climb up a ladder, you must begin at the bottom, and ascend up step by step, until you arrive at the top; and so it is with the principles of the Gospel—you must begin with the first, and go on until you learn all the principles of exaltation. But it will be a great while after you have passed through the veil before you will have learned them. It is not all to be comprehended in this world; it will be a great work to learn our salvation and exaltation even beyond the grave." (*Teachings of the Prophet Joseph Smith*, p. 348.)

SEATTLE TEMPLE

Bless, we pray thee, the presidency of this temple and the matron and all the officiators herein. Help them to create a sublime and holy atmosphere so that all ordinances may be performed with love and a sweet, spiritual tone that will cause the members to greatly desire to be here, and to return again and again.

We remember before thee, our Father, the youth of Zion. Bear them up that they shall not falter in defending truth and right. Help them to be clean and worthy and instill in them a desire for eternal marriage in thy holy temple.

Our Beloved Father, bless the daughters of Zion, we pray thee. Pour out precious gifts of wisdom, faith, and knowledge upon them.

◆

From the dedicatory prayer by
Spencer W. Kimball
November 17–21, 1980

21

That Which Would Be
of Most Worth

◆

In the early days of the Church, John Whitmer prayed many times to the Lord desiring to know that which would be of the most worth to him. The Lord gave him the answer: "That you may bring souls unto me, that you may rest with them in the kingdom of my Father." (D&C 16:6.)

We usually determine how we will spend our time by what our reward will be. A person goes to work five days a week because it gives him the security of a consistent income. The entrepreneur starts a business because it fulfills his desire to be creative and independent. The politician runs for political office because it satisfies his desire to attain recognition and influence among his fellow men. The alcoholic surrenders himself to his appetite because it enables him to escape from reality. It is a rare and unique person who loses himself in the service of others without the expectation of worldly remuneration of some sort.

When I was a young boy, a widow lived in a humble home on Canyon Road in Salt Lake City. Her income was meager—so small that it could hardly support one person—yet for years she took the sick, bedridden, and destitute who were without family and means and nursed them back to good health. Periodically my mother would have me deliver freshly baked bread and other necessities to her small apartment, and at Christmastime a box of groceries. Few people knew of the selfless Christian service that this wonderful widow rendered to the sick and needy. There was no tooting of horns nor blowing of whistles. There were no newspaper articles nor acknowledgments. Her work of mercy was known only to her, the Lord, and a few others. I have often thought she was the closest thing to an angel I ever saw.

We have a tendency to ask ourselves, "What will it do for me if I go to the temple?" We talk about how happy they are who attend and work in the temple, and indeed they are. We talk of the Holy Spirit penetrating our souls as we perform the ordinances by proxy for our progenitors and others. We talk of the peace that comes into our minds and hearts as we bask in the celestial atmosphere of the temple. We read and ponder the scriptures and attend the temple that an understanding of the knowledge of eternity might distill upon us. But too seldom do we consider the supernal service that temple activity renders to those in the spirit world who cannot do for themselves what we alone are able to do for them.

Speaking of the work performed in the temples of the Lord, President Gordon B. Hinckley said, "This is the greatest selfless act of Christian service that we can perform in this mortal life." (Address, Dedication of Taiwan Temple, November 1984.) When we come to the temple we have the opportunity of performing selfless Christian service for those who cannot help themselves. We extend the opportunity of exaltation to another of God's children who has preceded us.

Some want to give themselves to something great. Joseph Smith said, "The greatest responsibility in this world, that God has laid upon us, is to seek after our dead." (*Teachings of the Prophet Joseph Smith, p. 356.)* "This doctrine was the burden of the scriptures. Those Saints who neglect it in behalf of their deceased relatives, do it at the peril of their own salvation." (*HC* 4:426.)

"And now, my dearly beloved brethren and sisters, let me assure you that these are principles in relation to the dead and the living that cannot be lightly passed over, as pertaining to our salvation. For their salvation is necessary and essential to our salvation, as Paul says concerning the fathers—that they without us cannot be made perfect—neither can we without our dead be made perfect." (D&C 128:15.)

The Savior taught:

> Then shall the King say unto them on his right hand, Come, ye blessed of my Father, inherit the kingdom prepared for you from the foundation of the world: for I was an hungred, and ye gave me meat: I was thirsty, and ye gave me drink: I was a stranger, and ye took me in: naked, and ye clothed me: I was sick, and ye visited me: I was in prison, and ye came unto me.
>
> Then shall the righteous answer him, saying, Lord, when saw we thee an hungred, and fed thee? or thirsty, and gave thee drink? When saw we thee a stranger, and took thee in? or naked, and clothed thee? Or when saw we thee sick, or in prison, and came unto thee?

And the King shall answer and say unto them, Verily I say unto you, inasmuch as ye have done it unto one of the least of these my brethren, ye have done it unto me. (Matthew 25:34–40.)

To paraphrase John F. Kennedy's words, let us not ask what temple service can do for us, but what we can do for our progenitors and others through temple worship—else "the whole earth would be utterly wasted at his coming." (D&C 2:3.)

JORDAN RIVER TEMPLE

May each contributor, whether of money or services or goods, rejoice in the opportunity to assist in thy holy work. May they be assured of the gratitude of those uncounted millions who have passed beyond this life, for whom the prison doors may now be opened and deliverance proclaimed. . . .

We humbly pray Father, that thou wilt accept this holy edifice. Pour out thy blessings upon it, as a house in which thou wilt come and in which thy Spirit will direct all that is done, that it may be acceptable unto thee.

————————◆————————

From the dedicatory prayer by
Marion G. Romney
November 16–20, 1981

22
The Quest for Happiness

◆

Much has been written and said about the Beatitudes. They have deep spiritual significance and are accepted as an example of masterful literary expression. The Savior was speaking to his disciples when he taught the Beatitudes. They represent a treasured utterance that teaches a person how he can become like Him. The last verse of the chapter containing the Beatitudes reveals his objective: "Therefore I would that ye should be perfect even as I, or your Father who is in heaven is perfect." (3 Nephi 12:48; see also Matthew 5:48.) The Beatitudes are a formula that if followed will take us from where we are to where the Savior wants us to be. They are interrelated and represent successive steps that one must take to reach the eternal objective of perfection that we must pursue in this life or the opportunity will be lost.

"Yea, blessed are the poor in spirit who come unto me, for theirs is the kingdom of heaven." As a first step one must overcome unrighteous or worldly pride and submit himself to the will of the Lord. When he persists in walking in his own way the other steps of the formula are of no avail. He must first humble himself before the Lord, come unto him, and be willing to follow him. This is a matter of attitude.

"And again, blessed are all they that mourn, for they shall be comforted." The Apostle Paul speaks of a godly sorrow for sin. This is essential for further progress. The process of repentance begins and the Lord gives assurance that such can lead to comfort and inner peace.

"And blessed are the meek, for they shall inherit the earth." The Lord said to the elders of his Church whom he appointed, "Ye are not sent forth to be taught, but to teach the children of men the things which I have put into your hands by the power of my Spirit." (D&C 43:15.) A person who is meek is teachable. Only those who are willing to listen can learn and progress.

"And blessed are all they who do hunger and thirst after righteousness, for they shall be filled with the Holy Ghost." To understand the gospel of Jesus Christ one must seek truth and have a desire to learn. The greater the desire the greater the reward, for to mortal men knowledge and understanding are limitless. The truths of the gospel are only understood through the Holy Ghost, which is promised to those who seek truth by study and prayer.

"And blessed are the merciful, for they shall obtain mercy." As one begins to understand the gospel he becomes more interested in helping other people both living and dead. This gospel is the greatest work of mercy the world has ever known. When we are merciful to others, the Lord is merciful to us.

"And blessed are all the pure in heart, for they shall see God." The reward for merciful service is purity of heart. One of the definitions of the word *see* in Webster's Dictionary is "to understand." Purity of heart enables one to better understand and to come to know God, which brings life eternal; for the Savior said, "And this is life eternal, that they might know thee the only true god, and Jesus Christ, whom thou hast sent." (John 17:3.)

"And blessed are all the peacemakers, for they shall be called the children of God." The by-product of purity of heart is inner peace—peace of mind and peace in the heart for which people of the world so desperately strive but seldom attain. Inner peace leads to a quest for peace in the home, peace in the community, peace in the nation, and peace in the world.

"And blessed are all they who are persecuted for my name's sake, for theirs is the kingdom of heaven. And blessed are ye when men shall revile you and persecute, and shall say all manner of evil against you falsely, for my sake, for ye shall have great joy and be exceeding glad, for great shall be your reward in heaven; for so persecuted they the prophets who were before you." (3 Nephi 12:3–12.) Inner peace enables one to withstand the persecution that often plagues those who sustain righteous principles.

Then the Lord tells us what kind of men we ought to be—that we should be willing to sustain righteousness and not be as salt which has lost its savor and is "good for nothing, but to be cast out and to be trodden under foot of men." Rather, we should let our "light so shine before this people, that they may see [our] good works and glorify [our] Father who is in heaven." (3 Nephi 12:13, 16.)

For those who serve mercifully in the temple of the Lord, the goal is the perfection spoken of in the Beatitudes. Temple blessings and temple service assist them to attain to this quality of life whether in this life or in the life hereafter. Sacred covenants are made with the Lord to help them remain free from sin and the stains of worldliness. His ways lead to exaltation if they remain faithful to the covenants made with the Lord in the temple.

All who are striving to do what is right and follow the Savior are his disciples. All who are striving to live according to the Beatitudes, regardless of how far they have progressed, have the same objective. Therefore, it behooves us to be understanding of one another, reaching out with a helping hand to build and strengthen our fellow men. More particularly, we should help those who have lost their way to find the path, take the first step, and progress toward the goal the Savior has set for us. If we do so, our lives will be more meaningful, joy and happiness will be our reward, and we too will become saviors of men.

We are in the business of building people. We should lift people up and never push them down. The further we progress toward the objective, the more important it is that we have understanding hearts and helping hands. This is the great work of the Master, whom we should and must emulate if we are to succeed in our strivings and quest for eternal life and celestial glory.

ATLANTA GEORGIA TEMPLE

May all who enter these holy precincts feel of thy Spirit and be bathed in its marvelous, sanctifying influence. May they come . . . in a spirit of love and dedication.

May the very presence of this temple in the midst of thy people become a reminder of the sacred and eternal covenants made with thee. May they strive more diligently to banish from their lives those elements which are inconsistent with the covenants they have made with thee.

May all who enter its portals realize that they are entering thy house as thy guest, and conduct themselves always with reverence and respect and love for thee.

◆

From the dedicatory prayer by
Gordon B. Hinckley
June 1–4, 1983

23

The Spirit of Temple Service

◆

Recently, I spoke to an ordinance worker in the temple. Her face was radiant. She looked like an angel in her beautiful white dress. I said to her, ''Why does everyone in the temple look so happy?'' She answered, ''Because they are happy.'' That seemed a most appropriate response. Those who serve in the temple are happy people and are generous in expressing the joy they receive in temple service.

The spirit in the temple is beautiful. The atmosphere is one of love, concern, and caring. Temple workers strive to perform each temple ordinance with exactness and to maintain a standard of excellence worthy of the Savior's presence. A quiet dignity prevails that promotes reverence, and a warm, friendly atmosphere brings joy to each heart. Temple workers pride themselves in being respectful, kind, and considerate to all who enter the portals.

One temple worker with whom I am acquainted suffers from diabetes. His condition is so serious that one leg has been amputated to the knee and the other is deteriorating, yet he continues to come to the temple regularly to fulfill his assignment. In the process he has developed unusual spiritual strength. When he prays publicly, he talks to the Lord as though he were face to face with Him. When he enters the temple, he radiates a spirituality that raises the spirits of all with whom he comes in contact. The temple workers hold him in love, respect, and even veneration.

Recently, another temple worker I know offered a benediction at a meeting in his stake. His prayer took the form of a testimonial. He said, ''When I enter the temple, my aches and pains disappear. When I leave the temple, my aches and pains return.''

Elder Melvin J. Ballard wrote, ''When you are in the sacred walls of these buildings, where you are entitled to the Spirit of the Lord, in the silent moments the answer will come. Many of you will be healed in your bodies by the power and influence that you will feel in these holy places. I have never, from the time I was a child, passed through the doors of a temple that I have not felt the heavenly spirit of that place. There is something comforting and uplifting about it." (*Melvin J. Ballard, Crusader for Righteousness*, pp. 251–52.)

A mother of four children, who lived at a location remote from the temple, was suffering with cancer. Even though she was terminally ill, she wanted to visit the temple once more. The family drove more than a hundred miles, took a one-and-a-half hour ferry ride, and then drove for another one and a half hours to the temple. She brought with her two oxygen tanks, a small convenient one to carry with her during the temple session and a large one for refills. During the session everyone was cooperative and took special care in looking after her every need. When she left the temple, workers with tears in their eyes bade her farewell. She returned home with an inner peace that transcended her discomfort. She died soon thereafter. Her husband and children return to the temple when opportunity permits, the children to serve as proxies for baptisms and the father to serve as a proxy for endowments.

A widow with limited means comes to serve in the temple one week each month. She boards a bus at her hometown and travels forty miles to a central city. Next, she boards another bus and travels two hundred miles to a city near the temple and then still another bus for ten miles to the bus stop near the temple. She then carries two suitcases for two blocks to her lodging, one filled with clothes and the other filled with food for the week. She has just enough to pay these costs and get along financially.

Coming to the temple is the joy of her life. Her clothes are worn and threadbare. Outside the temple her dress portrays her frugality, but when she enters the temple and dons her white clothing she has the appearance of a beautiful angel. One cannot distinguish her from the most wealthy person in the temple. In the temple all are wealthy. Last winter one of the temple workers saw this wonderful sister leaving the temple at day's end in her thin and worn coat. She removed her own expensive coat and placed it around her shoulders. It was a perfect fit. She insisted that it be hers. Reluctant at first, she finally accepted it and walked into the cold evening weather warm, attractive, and grateful. Two of God's choice daughters retired that evening, each grateful for one another and for the good things the Lord had provided.

Another temple worker, seeing this sister's plight, has invited her to stay in her home when she comes to serve in the temple. This saves her the cost of housing and food for the week and enables her to use her limited income to care more adequately for her other needs. Such care and concern typifies the spirit of temple service.

Elder George F. Richards wrote:

> Those who have never done temple work cannot appreciate its significance; and its full import, perhaps, is never fully grasped by any mortal. . . .
>
> This work naturally makes one forget self. People thus engaged follow, in a measure, the example of our Savior, by doing for others the things they cannot do for themselves. . . .
>
> To a careful observer, doubtful as to the value of temple work, the abundant evidences of spiritual growth of those who engage in it is most convincing. There is a calm and sweet serenity about them which is indeed heavenly. ("Latter-day Temples," *Improvement Era*, May 1930, p. 473.)

King David asked, "Who shall stand in his holy place?" And then he answered his own question: "He that hath clean hands, and a pure heart; who hath not lifted up his soul unto vanity, nor sworn deceitfully. He shall receive the blessing from the Lord, and righteousness from the God of his salvation." (Psalm 24:3–5.)

APIA SAMOA TEMPLE

Wilt thou open the way for thy people to seek out the records of their forebears that they may serve as saviors on Mount Zion in opening the prison doors of those whose progress has been stopped beyond the veil, that these may now become the beneficiaries of the sacred ordinances of thy holy house, and go forward on the way to eternal life and exaltation in thy presence.

◆

From the dedicatory prayer by
Gordon B. Hinckley
August 5–6, 1983

24
Security in a World of Turmoil

◆

As evidenced by the violence, atrocities, wars, famine, devastation, and destructive forces of nature reported by the news media each day, we are obviously living in a time of confusion. The Lord has warned us of these days, declaring that the troubles in the world will cause men's hearts to fail them. It appears that matters will get worse before they get better. All of this creates feelings of insecurity resulting in even greater confusion evidenced by marital problems, drug abuse, intolerance, distrust, lawlessness, delinquency, and unhappy homes. If men, women, and children ever needed an anchor to attain security, they need it in today's world of turmoil.

Whenever a person attends more than one temple session consecutively, something very special happens. It often takes the first session to clear worldly thoughts and concerns from his mind. By the time he has completed the second session, lights seem brighter, white seems whiter, troubles seem lighter, and solutions to problems become more apparent. It is an exhilarating experience.

Temple worship does much to stabilize our lives. A sweet, peaceful feeling comes from this service that can be found nowhere else. The spirit emanating from the temple and carried home by those participating in temple worship results in a spiritual enrichment of the home. The family and loved ones get along better. Love for one another becomes more intense. There is less contention. A greater feeling of satisfaction and accomplishment envelops us. One's testimony of the gospel becomes stronger and more deeply anchored in the soul. Carnal thoughts and worldly influences are more easily overcome. Feelings of celestial satisfaction emanate from within. Anticipation of temple worship makes life more worthwhile. Feelings and attitudes of depression, loneliness, and discouragement are overcome or markedly reduced. Temple blessings build the spirit and soul to overcome insecurity without the use of tranquilizers, drugs, and medicine. This is the Lord's prescription, which builds the immune system and enables the mind and body of the individual to maintain or restore health and vigor.

Elder John A. Widtsoe said: "Temples are for the benefit and enlightenment of the members of the Church. In them are revealed the keys of the Priesthood, and there power is given men 'from on high' to meet the many issues of life. There men may commune with the forces of heaven, until doubt and questioning are replaced by knowledge and certainty. . . . Those who have received with open hearts the blessings of the temple go out with increased power and a new understanding of life's problems." ("The House of the Lord," *Improvement Era*, April 1936, p. 228.)

The Lord has said, "If ye are prepared ye shall not fear." (D&C 38:30.) To obtain the most out of a temple visit a person must prepare himself. Those who enter the temple and desire to obtain most from the experience must seek to purify their hearts in preparation. Only those who do so share fully in the blessings that flow from the temple. Time spent in the temple helps us to prepare ourselves spiritually for future visits.

Elder John A. Widtsoe wrote: "Spiritual power is generated within temple walls, and sent out to bless the world. Light from the house of the Lord illumines every home within the Church fitted for its reception by participation in temple privileges." ("The House of the Lord," *Improvement Era*, April 1936, p. 228.)

Elder Vaughn J. Featherstone said, "I promise you that all who faithfully attend to temple work will be blessed beyond measure—your families will draw closer to the Lord, unseen angels will watch over your loved ones when satanic forces tempt them, the veil will be thin, and great spiritual experiences will distill upon this people." (Mt. Vernon Washington Stake Conference, June 1985.)

"Going to the temple will greatly enhance the perfecting of the Saints and relieve their social problems as well as fortify their faith." (W. Grant Bangerter, First Quorum of the Seventy Meeting Address, 5 February 1986.)

Most of our problems come from within our own minds. As the Lord has counseled, we should strip ourselves from jealousies and fears, and humble ourselves before him. (See D&C 67:10.) Those who enter the temple worthily and have prepared themselves find that small and petty problems disappear or are minimized. The larger ones often become solvable or the individual is strengthened to enable him to endure his afflictions with a peace of mind that transcends his concerns.

By coming to the temple one can gain a better perspective of life. The young, the old, the lame, the halt, the blind, the rich, the poor, the healthy, the infirm—all are alike in the house of the Lord. The healthy feel healthier, the wealthy feel more humble, many of the infirm are relieved from their suffering, the lame often become more mobile. The atmosphere is celestial, for there is no aspiring, no fault finding, no criticism, no tale bearing. Love prevails, happiness reigns, joy is full, and life is enriched. The nobleness of men and women blossoms in the glory that prevails within the sacred walls of the temple.

Security comes from within. It is not the financial nor the social *altitude* we attain in this life, but the uplifting *attitude* for which we strive in the temple that qualifies us to receive blessings of inner peace and a feeling of security in a troubled world.

NUKU'ALOFA TONGA TEMPLE

We ask that thou wilt accept this temple as the
gift of thy people presented unto thee with love
for the accomplishment of thy holy purposes
with reference to thy children. It is thy house.
It is the house of thy Son. May it always be
held in reverence by thy people.

———————————— ◆ ————————————

From the dedicatory prayer by
Gordon B. Hinckley
August 9–11, 1983

25

After Much Tribulation
Come the Blessings

◆

The Lord said, "My people must be tried in all things, that they may be prepared to receive the glory that I have for them, even the glory of Zion; and he that will not bear chastisement is not worthy of my kingdom." (D&C 136:31.)

Many times during our lives we face a serious problem of some sort that gives us great concern. We are inclined to think that we are the only ones who have problems and we ask ourselves, "Why me?" The fact is everyone has problems. Dr. Norman Vincent Peale facetiously said, "If you don't have a problem, go out and get one." Then he explained that the process of overcoming problems builds and strengthens the individual.

In the sacramental prayer we pray to our Father in Heaven professing that we are willing to take upon ourselves the name of Jesus Christ. What does it mean to take upon ourselves his name? Jesus answered the question when he said, "Come follow me." To follow him means to keep his commandments and strive to emulate him. We try to walk in his footsteps. This not only means to be willing to do what he did, but to go where he went. And where did he go? As he bid farewell to his disciples at the last supper he said: "In my Father's house are many mansions: if it were not so, I would have told you. I go to prepare a place for you. And if I go and prepare a place for you, I will come again, and receive you unto myself; that where I am, there ye may be also." (John 14:2–3.)

By following him we can share the glory of the Father. But this is not the only place he went following the Last Supper. He also went to his Gethsemane. He went below all things so that he might rise above all things. To enjoy the sweet, we too must first taste the bitter. The sacramental prayer does not require us to follow Jesus through his Gethsemane, but rather to be willing to do so. We are required, however, to go through our own Gethsemanes and remain faithful so that we too might rise above all things even as he has done. We cannot share in the glory of the Father without proving ourselves by remaining faithful as we go through the anxieties and sufferings that accompany mortal life.

Willingness to follow the Savior is the real test. Here is where agency comes into effect. We have our agency to follow the Savior, to follow some other person, or to follow after our own will. The Lord said that his anger is kindled against the inhabitants of the world, "for they have strayed from mine ordinances, and have broken mine everlasting covenant; they seek not the Lord to establish his righteousness, but every man walketh in his own way, and after the image of his own god, whose image is in the likeness of the world, and whose substance is that of an idol, which waxeth old and shall perish in Babylon, even Babylon the great, which shall fall." (D&C 1:15–16.) Joshua expressed his preference and willingness when he said, "Choose you this day whom ye will serve; . . . but as for me and my house, we will serve the Lord." (Joshua 24:15.)

In speaking of the Saints in Missouri, the Lord said: "They were slow to hearken unto the voice of the Lord their God; therefore, the Lord their God is slow to hearken unto their prayers, to answer them in the day of their trouble. In the day of their peace they esteemed lightly my counsel; but, in the day of their trouble, of necessity they feel after me. . . . Notwithstanding their sins, my bowels are filled with compassion towards them." (D&C 101:7–9.) In showing that compassion he said: "I, the Lord, have suffered the affliction to come upon them, wherewith they have been afflicted, in consequence of their transgressions; yet I will own them, and they shall be mine in that day when I shall come to make up my jewels. Therefore, they must needs be chastened and tried, even as Abraham, who was commanded to offer up his only son. For all those who will not endure chastening, but deny me, cannot be sanctified." (D&C 101:2–5.)

To assist us to sail our ship safely into the harbor of eternal life, the Lord has provided the temple, which is designed to prepare his children for celestial living. Each ordinance in the temple must be sealed by the Holy Spirit of promise, which is earned as we remain faithful to the covenants we have made with the Lord in his holy temple.

Regular visits to the temple build a greater understanding of eternal principles and a greater resolve to discipline ourselves to follow him. Regular visits to the temple bring spiritual refreshment, inner peace, and enlightenment from God that prepares us for future realms. Regular visits to the temple release us from earthly stains and relieve us from worldly concerns. Regular visits to the temple enable us to be more valiant and skillful as we guide our ships through the rocky course of mortality. "For after much tribulation come the blessings. Wherefore the day cometh that ye shall be crowned with much glory." (D&C 58:4.)

SANTIAGO CHILE TEMPLE

Bless thy work upon this great continent of South America which is part of the land of Zion. Bless thy work in this nation of Chile. May all that has been done in the past be but a prologue to a far greater work in the future. May thy people be recognized for the virtue of their lives.

Now, Almighty God, we pray that thy Saints may find favor in thy sight, that faith shall grow in the hearts of thy people, that love shall abound in their homes, that the spirit of Zion may be found among them and that they shall be a blessed and happy people. Prosper them in their labors. Open the windows of heaven and pour out blessings upon the faithful that there shall not be room enough to receive them.

◆

From the dedicatory prayer by
Gordon B. Hinckley
September 15–17, 1983

26

Patience Has Its Reward

♦

The Lord has instructed us that "all covenants, contracts, bonds, obligations . . . or expectations, that are not made and entered into and sealed by the Holy Spirit of promise, of him who is anointed, both as well for time and for all eternity . . . are of no efficacy, virtue, or force in and after the resurrection from the dead; for all contracts that are not made unto this end have an end when men are dead." (D&C 132:7.)

He has also taught us that "in the celestial glory there are three heavens or degrees; and in order to obtain the highest, a man must enter into this order of the priesthood (meaning the new and ever-lasting covenant of marriage); and if he does not, he cannot obtain it. He may enter into the other, but that is the end of his kingdom; he cannot have an increase." (D&C 131:1–4.)

We have many single worthy women in the Church who, real-izing the significance of the above, are frustrated because they are unable to find a companion with whom they can unite in celestial marriage. Some may have been divorced through no fault of their own. Others have never had the privilege of temple marriage. Women in such circumstances include some of the most noble spir-its of our Heavenly Father. Many become discouraged and feel that justice has not prevailed in their situation.

Some say that finding a husband is not within the power of a young lady. What the Lord expects of each of his daughters is that she seek out those opportunities and make those choices that will keep her worthy of returning to his presence. "For if you will," the Lord says, "that I give unto you a place in the celestial world, you must prepare youselves by doing the things which I have com-manded you and required of you." (D&C 78:7.)

The Lord requires obedience to his principles and has made us promises connected thereto, such as these: "Draw near unto me and I will draw near unto you; seek me diligently and ye shall find me; ask, and ye shall receive; knock, and it shall be opened unto you. Whatsoever ye ask the Father in my name it shall be given unto you, that is expedient for you; and if ye ask anything that is not expedient for you, it shall turn unto your condemnation." (D&C 88:63–65.) "And if your eye be single to my glory, your whole bodies shall be filled with light, and there shall be no darkness in you. . . . Therefore, sanctify yourselves that your minds become single to God, and the days will come that you shall see him; for he will unveil his face unto you, and it shall be in his own time, and in his own way, and according to his own will." (D&C 88:67–68.) The Lord can accomplish this not only through a personal appearance but also by giving us revelation, by enabling us to see with our minds—which can be more assuring than normal sight. Thus, our minds, hearts, and souls can be put to rest about the matters that deeply concern us.

The prophet Alma said that God "granteth unto men according to their desire. . . . He that knoweth not good from evil is blameless; but he that knoweth good and evil, to him it is given according to his desires, whether he desireth good or evil, life or death, joy or remorse of conscience." (Alma 29:4–5.)

President Spencer W. Kimball said regarding this matter, "There is a great and grand principle involved here. Just as those that do not hear the gospel in this life, but who would have received it with all their hearts had they heard it, will be given the fulness of the gospel blessings in the next world—so too, the women of the Church who do not in this life have the privileges and blessings of a temple marriage, through no fault of their own, who would have responded if they had an appropriate opportunity—will receive all those blessings in the world to come." (Women's Fireside Address, 16 September 1978.)

President Harold B. Lee, speaking of this same principle as relating to young men, said, "Likewise, . . . young men who may lose [their] lives in a terrible conflict before [they] have had an opportunity for marriage, the Lord knows the intents of [their] hearts and in his own time will reward [them] with opportunities made possible through temple ordinances instituted in the Church for that purpose." (*Youth and the Church*, p. 129.)

The temple not only gives opportunity for eternal blessings through vicarious service to those who do not have proper opportunities in this life but also serves as a place of learning and a place of understanding, which becomes a stepping-stone during our sojourn in mortality to prepare us for celestial glory. Just as one enters a university to prepare himself for commencement of life after graduation, so we can enter the temple in this life and prepare ourselves for commencement of life after graduation from mortality where we will receive the righteous desires of our hearts and other wondrous blessings the Lord has in store for the faithful.

In a school of higher learning, we do not attend just one class and consider ourselves qualified for commencement. We attend classes regularly and repeatedly until the knowledge and understanding of the subject is inculcated into our minds. Likewise, we must not assume that by attending one session of the temple we have properly prepared ourselves for commencement into the next life. In the temple we are taught by the Holy Spirit. We can learn more important things from temple attendance when we properly prepare ourselves than we can in a university. Regular temple attendance will prepare us for commencement into a realm of inexpressible joy and peace where the righteous desires of our hearts will be fulfilled.

God will grant the desires of the heart of a righteous person when he or she asks in prayer—but in his own way and in his own time. What specific plans he has for each of us who remain faithful we know not. Therefore, it behooves us to remain faithful, serve him loyally, ask him for the righteous desires of our hearts, and be patient even into eternity.

PAPEETE TAHITI TEMPLE

We look back with appreciation to the Prophet Joseph Smith to whom thou didst reveal thyself with thy Son. . . .

Since that time there have been seasons of prosperity and seasons when problems were many and the harvest was lean. But through all of these years thy work has grown as with faith thy servants have labored among the Tahitian people and found those who have been touched by the Spirit and who have come into the fold of the Church. There is now strength and maturity among the many thousands of the Saints of French Polynesia, for which we express gratitude unto thee. As a capstone to all of this effort we now have this beautiful and sacred house to present unto thee.

We dedicate it as the house of the Lord with holiness unto thee, to be used by thy worthy Saints to assist in bringing to pass the immortality and eternal life of thy sons and daughters.

◆

From the dedicatory prayer by
Gordon B. Hinckley
October 27–29, 1983

27

Building Moral Strength

◆

Much has been said in recent years about the new morality. Those who would compromise traditional standards have taken license to establish new moral values for society. Pornography is tolerated, infidelity is accepted, adultery is rampant, and the distribution of drugs has moved from the pharmacy to the campus and city streets. College students are exposed to new concepts of morality from men who are determined to change accepted standards. High school students and younger children are influenced by those who prey upon unshielded adolescence.

There is only one who has the authority to establish true standards of morality by which we will be judged. This is he who created the world. Jesus Christ is the standard bearer. He is the lawmaker. He never changes. His standards are the same yesterday, today, and tomorrow. Three and one-half thousand years ago he gave Moses the Ten Commandments, which are just as apropos today as they were then.

In 1831 the Lord revealed the following to his Saints through the Prophet Joseph Smith: ''Inasmuch as you strip yourselves from jealousies and fears, and humble yourselves before me . . . the veil shall be rent and you shall see me and know that I am—not with the carnal neither natural mind, but with the spiritual. For no man has seen God at any time in the flesh, except quickened by the Spirit of God. Neither can any natural man abide the presence of God, neither after the carnal mind.'' (D&C 67:10–12.)

While each person has but one mind he can use it in three different ways: carnally, naturally, and spiritually. We have our agency to develop whichever we desire; nevertheless, we are held responsible for the choice we make. We have communities of people in the world today who have chosen to use their carnal minds extensively. They excuse themselves by saying they were ''born that way''—but this is contrary to what the Lord teaches. There are those who develop their natural minds to the exclusion of the spiritual. This is prevalent in our schools of higher learning and also in our society as a whole. Members of the Church who exclude spiritual thoughts from their minds soon lose their testimonies. "For my thoughts are not your thoughts, neither are your ways my ways, saith the Lord. For as the heavens are higher than the earth, so are my ways higher than your ways, and my thoughts than your thoughts." (Isaiah 55:8-9.)

Fortunately, we have a sacred place where we can come to improve our spiritual minds and thus attain to a favorable balance between the spiritual and the natural. To qualify for entrance into the temple of the Lord, we must adhere to the moral values established by the Savior and cleanse ourselves from the influence of the carnal mind. "When you enter a holy temple, you are by that course gaining fellowship with the Saints in God's eternal kingdom, where time is no more. In the temples of your God you are endowed not with a rich legacy of worldly treasure, but with a wealth of eternal riches that are above price." (Harold B. Lee, "Enter a Holy Temple," *Improvement Era*, June 1967, p. 144.)

"The temple ceremonies are designed by a wise Heavenly Father who has revealed them to us in these last days as a guide and a protection throughout our lives, that you and I might not fail to merit exaltation in the celestial kingdom where God and Christ dwell." (Ibid.) "Temple experience . . . presents the broad, sweeping panorama of God's purposes relating to this earth. Once we have been through the temple (and we can return and refresh our memories) the events of life fit into the scheme of things. We can see in perspective where we are, and we can quickly see when we are off course." (Boyd K. Packer, *The Holy Temple*, p. 47.) President Spencer W. Kimball encouraged the Saints to attend the temple regularly and then gave this important message, "Nothing builds spirituality and our understanding of the priesthood principles more than regular temple attendance." ("Remember the Mission of the Church," *Ensign*, April 1982, pp. 4-5.)

The Lord said to us, "Wherefore, lift up your hearts and rejoice, and gird up your loins, and take upon you my whole armor, that ye may be able to withstand the evil day, having done all, that ye may be able to stand." (D&C 27:15.) As a consequence, we attain a better way of thinking and a better way of life for ourselves, which places us beyond the influence of the adversary; and we have a more refining influence upon our families, which promotes improved family relationships and a better community spirit.

Consider the words of Elder John A. Widtsoe: "Every time a person receives the temple endowment for another, he reviews the eternal journey of man, is reminded of the conditions of eternal progress and of his own covenants to obey God's law, is impressed anew with the necessity of making truth alive by use, and beholds again the glorious destiny of righteous man. His memory is refreshed, his conscience warned, his hopes lifted heavenward. Temple repetition is the mother of daily blessings. Wherever one turns, temple service profits those who perform it." ("The House of the Lord," *Improvement Era*, April 1936, p. 228.)

The contrast between the morality of the world and the morality of God is so striking as regards the journey, the destination, and the reward, that only those who have lost their spiritual orientation would vacillate in selecting the path that leads through the temple to eternal life.

MEXICO CITY TEMPLE

Bless thy Saints in this great land and those
from other lands who will use this temple. Most
have in their veins the blood of Father Lehi.
Thou hast kept thine ancient promises. Many
thousands ''that walked in darkness have seen
a great light.'' (Isaiah 9:2.)

May the harvest that we have witnessed here
foreshadow greater things to come as thy work
rolls on in power and majesty in this the dispensation of the fulness of times.

◆

From the dedicatory prayer by
Gordon B. Hinckley
December 2–4, 1983

28

Enoch and Zion—the Great Example

♦

"There is a strange thing in the land; a wild man hath come among us," the scriptures record of Enoch who lived in the days of Adam. (Moses 6:38.) Enoch had a vision in his youth in which the Lord commanded him to preach repentance to certain people who were wicked and had gone astray. He questioned the Lord as to the advisability of calling him, for he was young and slow of speech and because "all the people hate me," he said. Nevertheless the Lord told him to go forth and do as he was commanded "and no man shall pierce thee," the Lord promised. "Open thy mouth, and it shall be filled, and I will give thee utterance. . . . Say unto this people: Choose ye this day, to serve the Lord God who made you." (Moses 6:31–33.)

Enoch did as the Lord commanded. The Lord instructed him to go up on Mount Simeon where he talked with the Lord face to face. The Lord showed him many things and again instructed him to call the people to repentance.

> And so great was the faith of Enoch, that he led the people of God, and their enemies came to battle against them; and he spake the word of the Lord, and the earth trembled, and the mountains fled, even according to his command; and the rivers of water were turned out of their course, . . . and all nations feared greatly, so powerful was the word of Enoch, and so great was the power of the language which God had given him. . . .
>
> And from that time forth there were wars and bloodshed among them; but the Lord came and dwelt with his people, and they dwelt in righteousness. . . .
>
> And the Lord called his people Zion, because they were of one heart and one mind, and dwelt in righteousness; and there was no poor among them. . . .
>
> And it came to pass in his days, that he built a city that was called the City of Holiness, even Zion. . . .
>
> And lo, Zion, in process of time, was taken up into heaven. . . .

And Enoch beheld angels descending out of heaven, bearing testimony of the Father and Son; and the Holy Ghost fell on many, and they were caught up by the powers of heaven into Zion. (Moses 7:13–27.)

In his talk at the centennial of the Logan Temple, President Ezra Taft Benson explained that Enoch brought the Saints of his day into the presence of God by following the pattern set by Adam. "How did Adam bring his descendants into the presence of the Lord?" he queried. "The answer: Adam and his descendants entered into the priesthood order of God. Today we would say they went to the House of the Lord and received their blessings." ("What I Hope You Will Teach Your Children About the Temple," *Ensign*, August 1985, p. 9.)

It is worthy of note that Enoch lived in the early period of world history. Could it be that the Lord established the City of Zion at that particular time as an example for the inhabitants of the earth to emulate? The world today is not so different from that of Enoch's day, with wickedness and sin rampant among the people of the earth. There is a great need for society today to emulate the people of Enoch's city. In one of President Benson's conference addresses of April 1986 he said that human nature can be changed, human nature has been changed in the past, human nature can be changed in the future, and that human nature must be changed. The only way human nature can be changed is through Christ. If human nature does not change, then the world will be destroyed by its own filth.

Temples of the Lord are Christ centered and are a means of changing the carnal nature of man, not by their mere existence, but by members' qualifying themselves, coming to the temple and receiving their temple blessings, remaining faithful to the covenants made with the Lord in the temple, and returning regularly to be taught from on high. Each temple emanates light—even a spirit which, carried by those who participate in temple service, becomes a leavening influence in the home and in the communities where participants reside.

When members of the Church are active in *regular* temple service, their quality of life improves and the Spirit of the Lord is more abundant in the home. Sir Winston Churchill said that a nation is no stronger than its families. If we are to change human nature, we must first strengthen the families of the Church, which will in turn strengthen the nation in which we reside. The world can be changed by emulating Enoch and his people, who are the great example for us to follow.

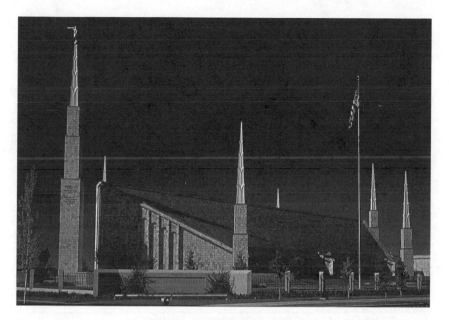

BOISE IDAHO TEMPLE

May thy faithful Saints of this and future generations look to this beautiful structure as a house to which they will be made welcome for their washings and anointings, for endowments and sealings, for instruction, for meditation, for worship, for the making of eternal covenants with thee, for inspiration and sanctification, as they serve unselfishly in assisting thee in bringing to pass thine eternal purposes for the salvation and exaltation of thy sons and daughters.

◆

From the dedicatory prayer by
Gordon B. Hinckley
May 25–30, 1984

29

Walking in the Lord's Way

◆

Every person has his agency and is entitled to his own opinions. However, opinions are not always well grounded. Greater credence is given to an opinion expressed by one who is considered to be an authority on a particular subject. In this age of commercialism we are bombarded with so many promotions that we become wary of statements made and philosophies advanced.

One day I was invited to be a participant in a panel at the University of Utah School of Business. The subject was "Our Moral Values." When I arrived I found there were four panelists: college professor, two Protestant ministers, and myself. As an introduction each participant was given five minutes to express himself about our moral values.

The first to speak was one of the ministers, who had several books on philosophy before him. He turned the pages and read what other men, whose opinion supposedly coincided with his, had written about the subject. The college professor did the same, which would have been expected. Then the second minister spoke using the same approach. The expressions of men who were considered to be authorities on the subject lent credence to their remarks.

It had been my plan to express personal opinions based on my own observations and experiences. I suddenly realized my planned remarks needed authenticity, so I turned to the book of Exodus in the Old Testament, read the Ten Commandments, and applied these words of God to the moral issues of the world today. As I pondered this experience in days that followed, I concluded that while I may not have impressed the academic mind I had the satisfaction of knowing that my comments were based on a higher authority than the remarks of my fellow panelists and thus had a more solid foundation.

The Lord says that his anger is kindled against the inhabitants of the world; "For . . . they seek not the Lord to establish his righteousness, but every man walketh in his own way, and after the

image of his own god, whose image is in the likeness of the world.''
(D&C 1:15-16.)

When a young man asked a meaningful question, a wise man
responded, "Have you searched the scriptures?" Answers to many
of life's questions are found in the scriptures. Ofttimes we appeal to
the Lord in earnest prayer about a specific problem and then in
searching the scriptures receive our answer from God through his
written word. When we learn the answer through expending the
effort to search, the lesson is more strongly emblazoned in our memory and thus our understanding is strengthened.

Many of us have strong opinions concerning philosophy, religion, and moral values but fail to search for the right answers from
the greatest authority of all, who has given us counsel through his
holy prophets since the world began.

God is the creator of the world and all things therein. He is the
official rule maker. He is all-wise. He is the great judge. He is all-
powerful. He knows all. He is above all. He is our counselor. We
have the assurance that his decisions are and will be just. He invites
us to "ask, and it shall be given you; seek, and ye shall find; knock,
and it shall be opened unto you: for every one that asketh receiveth;
and he that seeketh findeth; and to him that knocketh it shall be
opened." (Matthew 7:7-8.) We ask the Lord through sincere prayer.
Fasting makes us more resolute, and when we add fasting to prayer
we become more receptive to his answers through the quiet whisperings of the Holy Spirit. Gradually our thoughts become more
clear and our feelings deeper concerning answers to our questions.
We needn't rely on our own understanding but can draw on the
depths of knowledge of a wise Heavenly Father and friend who
loves each of us as we love our own children.

Service in the temple helps us to develop a close relationship
with God. It doesn't matter what kind of service one performs in
the temple—as an ordinance worker, a patron, or a volunteer on
the temple staff doing any one of a number of assignments that
must be accomplished for the temple to operate efficiently in a celestial atmosphere. There is opportunity for all who desire to serve
and enjoy the benefit that results from giving oneself to this sacred
work, which the Lord has decreed so vitally important to the welfare of mankind. One doesn't need to wait to be called to an assignment in the temple, but can serve as a proxy in behalf of one who
now resides in the spirit world who has not previously received his

or her temple blessings. The only requirement is holding a valid temple recommend, which can be received only by living in harmony with the commandments and the expectations of the Lord.

By receiving our own temple endowment, by remaining faithful to our temple covenants, and by returning to the temple regularly to perform this sacred merciful service, we may achieve purity of heart. The Savior said, "Blessed are the pure in heart: for they shall see God." (Matthew 5:8.) To see God may mean something different to different people; nevertheless, it is an experience that brings peace of mind, joy into one's heart, emotional stability to actions and attitudes, and love for one another that transcends those worldly cares that too often overcrowd our thoughts.

Temple service teaches one to walk in the footsteps of the Savior and to respond to his admonition, "Come follow me." In doing so we take a major step in preparing ourselves for the glory which our Father in Heaven has promised *those who endure in righteousness to the end*. Temple service builds commitment, dedication, resolve, and diligence. Temple service builds faith, hope, charity, and humility. Temple service builds love, brotherly kindness, knowledge, and virtue. Temple service builds thoughtfulness, gentleness, patience, and meekness. The pitfalls of walking in our own way are accordingly overcome. The book of Proverbs gives this sage advice: "Trust in the Lord with all thine heart; and lean not unto thine own understanding." (Proverbs 3:5.)

SYDNEY AUSTRALIA TEMPLE

May [this temple] . . . be as a beacon to thy Saints throughout the land. May it be as an anchor when the storms of life beat about them. May it be a place of holiness to which they may come, a house of sanctification, a house of prayer, a house of covenants.

May this temple with its grounds be a place of beauty to all who look upon it. May they be touched by thy Spirit as they do so, that there may come into their hearts a feeling of respect for thee and thy people, and an increase of love for thee, our God.

◆

From the dedicatory prayer by
Gordon B. Hinckley
September 20–23, 1984

30

A Family Can Be Forever

$\blacklozenge$

By being baptized, members of The Church of Jesus Christ of Latter-day Saints have already taken the first steps toward someday entering the celestial kingdom. But baptism alone is not enough to enable a complete family to be together in the kingdom of heaven.

God has revealed a great truth that is the key to a family's being together forever. He said, "In the celestial glory there are three heavens or degrees; and in order to obtain the highest, a man must enter into this order of the priesthood (meaning the new and everlasting covenant of marriage)." (D&C 131:1–2.)

God intended marriages to last forever; whenever the gospel has been on the earth, as it is now, the Lord has had agents to whom he has given power to bind on earth and seal eternally in heaven. (See Matthew 16:17–19; D&C 132:7.) Unless a marriage is performed in the temple by one who holds the proper authority, it ends when we die. Marriages performed in the temple in the new and everlasting covenant can last forever if the couple lives worthily.

After the date of their baptism, new members have at least a one-year waiting period to prepare to receive their temple blessings. Before a couple is sealed as husband and wife eternally, they receive their temple endowments. In the endowment a person receives information and knowledge about the Lord's purposes and plans and may qualify for special blessings from God based upon his faithfulness in keeping the commandments.

After a couple has received their endowments, they can be married and sealed together as husband and wife forever. A couple married by civil authority is married for this life only—that is, until death separates them. In the temple they will be sealed or bound together for all eternity, provided they remain worthy of this blessing.

After the couple is sealed, if they have children, the children may enter the sealing room in the temple and be sealed to their parents forever. When this is done, the family has the potential of becoming an eternal family. The family has received ordinances necessary for them to have eternal life with God the Father and his Son Jesus Christ and with those of their family who qualify for the highest degree of the celestial kingdom. Children born to parents who have been previously sealed in the temple are "born in the covenant" and are automatically sealed to their parents.

Family members must remember that they will receive these blessings only if they strive to live their lives in accord with the covenants they have made in the temple. At times members may feel that they are falling short of living as they know they should. All have continual need to repent. If we keep our lives in harmony with God's ways and demonstrate a sincere desire to keep his commandments, he will forgive us of our shortcomings and help us in our quest toward perfection.

Once a person is converted and joins the Church, he wants to share the gospel with his children, parents, and other relatives. If loved ones accept the gospel, they can be baptized, receive their endowments, and be sealed to their family. But what about family members, such as parents, grandparents, and other relatives who died before they found the truth? While they lived, these people were never baptized and never received the temple ordinances. How can they become part of their forever family?

At death our spirit continues to live. It goes to a place called the spirit world to await the resurrection. Just as there are missionaries here on earth teaching the gospel of Jesus Christ, there are also missionaries teaching that same gospel in the spirit world. Between the death of Jesus and his resurrection, he went to the spirit world and taught the gospel. (1 Peter 3:19–20, 4–6.) He appointed missionaries and sent them forth to teach the gospel to those who did not have the opportunity to accept it in this life. (D&C 138:29–37.)

These spirits can accept the gospel in the spirit world, but they cannot be baptized or receive the other saving ordinances there because these ordinances must be performed on this earth. Therefore, we who are living must perform these ordinances for them. To receive the saving ordinances for an ancestor, a member must know the ancestor's name and know when and where the ancestor was born, whom he married, when he was married, and where and when he died. To find this necessary data, we must gather information about our parents, grandparents, great-grandparents, and others. This searching is called genealogical research. As we discover this vital information about our ancestors, it should be recorded to show the family relationships. The information that uniquely identifies an individual may be recorded on a special form and sent to the genealogical service center that processes names for the temple. (Inquiry can be made to determine the location of the genealogical service center serving a particular temple.) Then an individual may serve as proxy for his deceased progenitor and receive temple ordinances vicariously in his behalf. Family members who have died and gone to the spirit world may have accepted the gospel already. If so, they too want to be baptized and receive their saving ordinances, which can only be performed here by those who are interested in their eternal welfare.

After members have been to the temple to receive their own endowments and the family has been sealed, they should return regularly to perform the saving ordinances for other ancestors and for others whose names are available at the temple. Returning to the temple often is a reminder of the great truths taught there and brings a refining influence into members' lives that prepares them for celestial life and celestial glory.

(The material in this chapter was initially prepared by the author for use in *A Lesson Book for New Members*, published in 1982.)

MANILA PHILIPPINES TEMPLE

Lift the blight of poverty from which so many suffer. Particularly bless thy faithful Saints who live honestly with thee in the payment of their tithes and offerings. Bless them that neither they nor their generations after them will go hungry, nor naked, nor without shelter from the storms that beat about them.

We thank thee for this beautiful edifice and for all who have worked to make it possible. May it stand as a pillar of truth and as an invitation to all who look upon it to learn of the purposes for which it has been created.

From the dedicatory prayer by
Gordon B. Hinckley
September 25–27, 1984

31

Building an Eternal Family

◆

The perception that families can be forever is an important concept in the gospel plan. The greatest source of happiness in this life comes from the love that prevails in a gospel-oriented family. A family that is well organized is more likely to be successful in its quest for unity, love, happiness, respect, and joy. "Our responsibility to organize our families at the immediate family level begins when a couple is married. The grandparent family organization develops as children from the immediate family marry and have children." (Ezra Taft Benson, "Worthy of All Acceptation," *Ensign*, November 1978, p. 30.)

The grandparent family is comprised of the oldest living grandparent in a specific line and his or her descendants. "Through such family organizations, every family in the Church should become actively involved in missionary work, . . . teaching the gospel, and cultural and social activities." (Ibid.)

The responsibility for temple and genealogical activity of the individual and his *immediate family* consists of: (1) receiving one's own temple blessings; (2) preparing family members to receive their temple blessings, including temple marriage; (3) ensuring that one's four-generation and extended genealogical family records have been submitted to the Ancestral File; (4) ensuring that one's family organizations are established and productive; (5) supporting grandparent and ancestral family organization projects and activities, including genealogical research; (6) serving as proxy in the temple regularly for those deceased ancestors whose saving ordinances have not been accomplished or for deceased individuals who have been identified through the name extraction program; (7) maintaining a personal record; and (8) preparing a personal history. Family home evening each week is an excellent time for the family to plan how the above can be accomplished.

The responsibility of a *grandparent organization* consists of: (1) organizing regular family temple activities; (2) preparing and submitting four-generation records to the Ancestral File; (3) coordinating family genealogical research beyond four generations in cooperation with ancestral family organizations; (4) ensuring that a family history is written; (5) promoting gospel scholarship within the family; (6) organizing family socials to strengthen and maintain family togetherness; and (7) developing the spiritual strength of family members through gospel study.

"*Ancestral organizations* exist . . . for the coordination of genealogical activity, which includes family histories. Once this function has been accomplished the ancestral family organization might well be dissolved, or at least reduced in importance, in favor of the immediate or grandparent organization." (Ibid, p. 31.) Ancestral family socials might be held every several years to preserve family heritage.

Temple and genealogical activities of a family unit might also include organizing family temple endowment sessions; organizing adults to do temple sealings and to perform washing, anointing, and clothing ordinances; and organizing youth of the family to perform vicarious baptisms for progenitors identified through genealogical research.

Missionary objectives might include (1) every son and grandson to fill a mission; (2) every adult couple to plan for mission service at the time of retirement; (3) to prepare friends and neighbors to receive the gospel; and (4) to love your neighbors.

Spiritual objectives might include (1) to hold family home evening meetings every week; (2) to organize a regular family scripture study period; (3) to establish family traditions that bring unity to the family, particularly these: every member of the family be active in Church, every young man fill a mission, every marriage be a temple marriage, every adult member attend the temple regularly, each family member maintain a personal relationship with God through prayer, and other traditions should be cultivated that build anticipation and interest in family togetherness; (4) to serve one another; and (5) to strive to reach a high standard of excellence in all that one does.

Temporal welfare objectives might include (1) to enthrone the principle of work as an essential to receiving joy and satisfaction; (2) to inculcate the principles of self-reliance in the family; (3) to encourage educational pursuits and excellence in scholarship; (4) to assist in finding and creating opportunities, when prudent, to help family members establish temporal independence; and (5) to promote physical fitness through exercise and proper eating habits.

The gospel of Jesus Christ is a family-centered plan. We can be exalted as families. While the celestial kingdom is available to single individuals, exaltation in that kingdom is not. If one does not have a fair opportunity to have an eternal companion in this life, a just God will see that justice is done and an opportunity given based upon one's faithfulness. Families are forever. Families should strive to be forever families to enable that same family sociality which exists here to continue hereafter, the realization of which will depend upon obedience to the covenants we make with the Lord in his house.

DALLAS TEXAS TEMPLE

Bless [the temple] that it may stand with dignity and strength as an expression of the dignity and strength of this, thy great latter-day work. Preserve it from wind and storm, and from the desecrating hands of those who are instruments of the adversary of truth. May their evil designs be stayed by thy mighty power, and wilt thou touch their hearts that they may see the error of their ways and cease from further efforts against thy work and thy people. May this beautiful temple, standing in this community, become a declaration to all who shall look upon it, of the faith of thy Saints in the revealed things of eternity, and may they be led to respect that which is sacred unto us, thy people.

◆

From the dedicatory prayer by
Gordon B. Hinckley
October 19–24, 1984

32

The Greatest Desire of One's Heart

◆

Recently we visited a branch of our family in a distant city where our fifteen-year-old granddaughter had lost her mother four years ago. I said to this young lady, "Do you know what I would like more than anything else in this whole world?"

She answered, "No, what?"

"I would like to have a forever family. Do you know what a forever family is?"

"Yes, it means we will be together forever."

"Do you know what we have to do to be a forever family?"

"We have to keep the commandments of the Lord."

"Do you think we can have a forever family?" I queried.

"You can count on me," she said.

Her ten-year-old brother, listening to our conversation, spoke up and said, "You can count on me too." My heart leaped for joy, for here was a commitment which, when honored by each of us, will bring about that which I desire most of all in and out of this world. We have four children and fourteen grandchildren and more grandchildren to come. Soon our children's children will have children and so our seed will expand and grow. It all started for us nearly fifty years ago, when my wife and I knelt at the altar in the temple and received the promise that we would have posterity extending into the eternities, if we remained faithful to the covenants we made with the Lord. Our family is now what brings us our greatest joy.

I dearly love and hold in veneration my mother and father. Their greatest desire is the same as mine. I have a great-grandmother whom I have never met, but I long to do so. She is probably as responsible for my being where I am today as anyone else.

In 1848 my grandfather was invited by his associates at the Bristol Iron Works in Bristol, England, to hear some missionaries from America who were scheduled to preach that evening at the town hall. He listened to their message, received a witness of its divinity, joined the Church, and in 1851 emigrated to America to join the body of the Saints in the Great Salt Lake Valley. He was obedient to the gospel message and sacrificed so that his posterity might be blessed by communion with the Saints. This had a dramatic influence on my destiny. I love and admire him and am anxious that his desire for an eternal family relationship be fulfilled.

In the ninety-eighth section of the Doctrine and Covenants the Lord appeals to us to "seek diligently to turn the hearts of the children to their fathers, and the hearts of the fathers to the children." (D&C 98:16.) The Prophet Joseph Smith said that the word *turn* in the scripture from Malachi should have been translated *seal* or *bind*. (*Teachings of the Prophet Joseph Smith*, p. 330.) The principle of turning the hearts of children and fathers to one another is of great importance and urgency.

The keys of the sealing power given to Joseph Smith and Oliver Cowdery on April 3, 1836, in the temple at Kirtland, Ohio, hold the power to seal husband to wife and children to parents, by which the family organization is made intact forever. In the process of preparing to and actually exercising these keys, the hearts of the children are turned to their fathers and the hearts of the fathers are turned to their children.

After the martyrdom of Joseph Smith, Brigham Young had a dream wherein he visited the Prophet Joseph and inquired of him concerning the law of adoption and the sealing principle. In response Joseph counseled, "Tell the brethren to keep the Spirit of the Lord and if they will, they will find themselves just as they were organized by our Father in Heaven before they came into the world. Our Father in Heaven organized the human family, but they are all (now) disorganized and in great confusion." Joseph then showed Brigham Young "how the human family were in the beginning. He saw where the priesthood had been taken from the earth, and how it had to be joined together so that there would be a perfect chain from Father Adam to his latest posterity." (*Millennial Star*, September 23, 1873, pp. 597–98.)

The sealing power of Elijah makes it possible to join families, generation to generation, back to the beginning. This is the great principle that will save the earth from being smitten with the curse of which Malachi spoke.

It is the ordinance of sealing that will enable our fifteen-year-old granddaughter, our ten-year-old grandson, their mother and father, and all the rest of our posterity and our progenitors to be united as a forever family in the eons to come, based upon our individual faithfulness. This should be our objective in all family and Church activities. The three-dimension mission of the Church— to proclaim the gospel of Jesus Christ to every nation, kindred, tongue, and people so as to prepare them to receive the ordinance of baptism and confirmation as members of the Church; to perfect the Saints by preparing them to receive the ordinances of the gospel and by instruction and discipline to gain exaltation; and to redeem the dead by performing vicarious ordinances of the gospel for those who have lived on the earth—describes what we must do and how we must do it to accomplish the Lord's objective of bringing eternal life to each individual who is willing to confirm his life to the will of God.

This process develops a spirit of family strength and solidarity and brings the human family into the condition prophesied by the Apostle Paul, "That in the dispensation of the fulness of times he might gather together in one all things in Christ, both which are in heaven, and which are on earth; even in him." (Ephesians 1:10.) Thus will the Lord in the fulness of times "gather together in one all things, both which are in heaven, and which are on earth." (D&C 27:13.)

TAIPEI TAIWAN TEMPLE

We thank thee for the firm foundation on which thy Church is now established in this part of the earth. We thank thee for this day when those who will use this temple may turn their hearts to their fathers, participating in this thy holy house in those ordinances which will make it possible for their deceased forebears to move forward on the way that leads to eternal life.

We ask that thou wilt preserve [the temple] . . . as thy house. May it be protected by thy power from any who would defile it. May it stand against the winds and the rains that beat upon it. May it be beautiful to all who see it and sacred to all who enter it.

◆

From the dedicatory prayer by
Gordon B. Hinckley
November 17–18, 1984

33

The Power to Bind in Heaven

◆

The dispensation of the fulness of times is a period in which the Saints of God are to prepare the kingdom of God on earth to receive the kingdom of Heaven at the second coming of the Savior, which is now near at hand. (See D&C 65.) In preparation for this great event the Melchizedek Priesthood was restored to the earth. In June of 1829 Peter, James, and John of New Testament times appeared to Joseph Smith and Oliver Cowdery and bestowed upon them the Melchizedek Priesthood, which is the authority to act in the name of God.

Certain priesthood keys were essential to the "restitution" spoken of by the Apostle Peter. (See Acts 3:19–21.) The prophet Elijah was the last Old Testament prophet to hold the keys of the power to bind in heaven that which is bound on earth. It was he who, upon the Mount of Transfiguration, bestowed upon Peter, James, and John the keys of that sealing power. (See Matthew 16:13–18; 17:1–9.) On April 3, 1836, Elijah appeared to Joseph Smith and Oliver Cowdery in the temple at Kirtland, Ohio and bestowed upon them these same keys—the sealing powers of the priesthood. (See D&C 110:13–16.)

There was a need for the Prophet Joseph Smith to have those keys, for the Church was embarking into a new era of ecclesiastical history, about which the Lord said, "I will gather together in one all things, both which are in heaven, and which are on earth; and also with all those whom my Father hath given me out of the world." (D&C 27:13–14.) In the epistle to the Ephesians, the Apostle Paul referred to this era in these words: "That in the dispensation of the fulness of times he might gather together in one all things in Christ, both which are in heaven, and which are on earth; even in him." (Ephesians 1:10.)

The Prophet Joseph Smith learned from the Lord that "it is necessary in the ushering in of the dispensation of the fulness of times, which dispensation is now beginning to usher in, that a whole and complete and perfect union, and welding together of dispensations, and keys, and powers, and glories should take place, and be revealed from the days of Adam even to the present time." (D&C 128:18.) Man of himself does not have the power to do this. The authority and power must come from God. This is the authority and power of which the Lord spoke when he gave a more correct translation of Malachi 4:5-6 through the angel Moroni to the Prophet Joseph Smith: "Behold, I will reveal unto you the Priesthood, by the hand of Elijah the prophet, before the coming of the great and dreadful day of the Lord. And he shall plant in the hearts of the children the promises made to the fathers, and the hearts of the children shall turn to their fathers. If it were not so, the whole earth would be utterly wasted at his coming." (D&C 2; JS—H 1:38-39.)

The power of godliness is manifest in the ordinances of the Melchizedek Priesthood (see D&C 84:20), without which the welding together in one could not take place. Temples have been built in this the dispensation of the fulness of times for the purpose of enabling this important part of the Lord's plan of salvation to be accomplished.

Under the authority of this priesthood, baptisms for the dead are performed in the baptismal fonts of temples of the Lord. Here our members serve as proxies for those who have died without an opportunity of hearing and accepting the gospel while in mortality. "You may think this . . . to be very particular (unique); but . . . it is only to answer the will of God, by conforming to the ordinance and preparation that the Lord ordained [set in order] and prepared before the foundation of the world, for the salvation of the dead who should die without a knowledge of the gospel." (D&C 128:5.)

> The faithful elders of this dispensation, when they depart from mortal life, continue their labors in the preaching of the gospel of repentance and redemption, through the sacrifice of the Only Begotten Son of God, among those who are in darkness and under the bondage of sin in the great world of the spirits of the dead.
>
> The dead who repent will be redeemed, through obedience to the ordinances of the house of God, and after they have paid the penalty of their transgressions, and are *washed clean*, shall receive a reward according to their works, for they are heirs of salvation. (D&C 138:57-59; italics added.)

To be washed clean, they must receive baptism by one having proper authority. But baptism is an earthly ordinance that must be performed on earth vicariously in their behalf. Baptism is the door to the celestial kingdom, and except a man be born of water and of the spirit he cannot gain entrance into that kingdom. (John 3:3-5.)

All other temple ordinances—washings, anointings, endowments, and sealings—are the door to exaltation in the celestial kingdom of God. "The dispensation of the fulness of times is the great era of vicarious ordinance work, a work which will continue during the millennial era until it has been performed for every living soul entitled to receive it." (Bruce R. McConkie, *Mormon Doctrine*, p. 73.)

According to President Joseph Fielding Smith, the keys of the sealing power are "the authorities which prepare men to enter the celestial kingdom and to be crowned as sons and heirs of God. These keys hold the power to seal husbands and wives for eternity as well as for time. They hold the power to seal children to parents, the key of adoption by which the family organization is made intact forever." (*Doctrines of Salvation*, 2:119.)

Many of the most spiritual and the most touching experiences in the temple are associated with the sealing of families. Not only are the hearts of the participants touched with a deep sense of gratitude to the Lord for the sealing of the family unit, but the hearts of those witnessing the sealing are touched with a feeling of love and appreciation to the Lord for the special spirit that prevails. As the father and the mother kneel at the altar and then together with the children—everyone dressed in white—the power of the priesthood is exercised in the sealing process. The family is not only sealed on earth but also sealed together in life after death, and not only is the sealing recorded on the temple records but also it is recorded in heaven. (D&C 128:8.) It must be kept in mind, however, that the validity of the temple ordinance is conditioned upon its ratification by the Holy Spirit of promise, which is earned through one's faithfulness to the covenants made in the temple. (See chapter 36.)

One day an Asian family came to the temple to be sealed. The family members were among the boat people who had fled from persecution in Vietnam. During their escape two of the children had perished. The rest of the family had been taken to a refugee camp and eventually brought to the United States. They were introduced to the gospel, accepted it, and were baptized, and had now come to the temple to receive their endowments and to be sealed as a family. The father and mother first knelt at the altar and were sealed as husband and wife for time and all eternity by one who had been given the authority to do so. The children were then brought into the sealing room. The family knelt around the altar with two other Asians acting as proxies for the deceased children and were sealed together as a family forever. When the ordinance was completed, the father stood up, gathered his wife and three children into his arms, and with tears rolling down his cheeks uttered, "You mine, you mine, you mine." And thus the power of the priesthood, which is the authority to seal in heaven that which is sealed on earth, was exercised to weld together one segment of God's family. This must be done for all who qualify through righteousness before the work is completed and it can be reported to the Father that "it is finished." (D&C 88:106.)

GUATEMALA CITY TEMPLE

Bless our land, O Father, this nation of Guatemala where stands thy holy house. May those who govern do so in righteousness. Bless them as they act to preserve the liberties and enhance the prosperity of the people. May there be peace in the land. May it be preserved from revolution and war. May there be freedom and equity under the law. May there be education and opportunity for all. May the forces of oppression and darkness be stayed by thy power, and may the light of truth shine over this Republic. So bless, Father, its neighbor nations that they may be preserved in independence and freedom.

◆

From the dedicatory prayer by
Gordon B. Hinckley
December 14–16, 1984

34
A Glimpse of Heaven

◆

One day while President Spencer W. Kimball was having his portrait painted, the artist was finding it difficult to get the expression he wanted on President Kimball's face. To solve the problem he asked, "Have you ever been to heaven?"

President Kimball's eyes narrowed in thought. In a few moments his countenance lightened as his mind settled on a recent experience.

Why, yes, Brother Richards, certainly. I had a glimpse of heaven just before coming to your studio . . . just an hour ago. It was in the holy temple across the way. The sealing room was shut off from the noisy world by its thick, white painted walls; the drapes, light and warm; the furniture, neat and dignified; the mirrors on two opposite walls seeming to take one in continuous likenesses on and on into infinity; and the beautiful stained glass window in front of me giving such a peaceful glow. All the people in the room were dressed in white. Here were peace and harmony and eager anticipation. A well-groomed young man and an exquisitely gowned woman, lovely beyond description, knelt across the altar. Authoritatively, I pronounced the heavenly ceremony which married and sealed them for eternity on earth and in the celestial worlds. The pure in heart were there. Heaven was there.

When the eternal marriage was solemnized, and as the subdued congratulations were extended, a happy father, radiant in his joy, offered his hand and said, "Brother Kimball, my wife and I are common people and have never been successful, but we are immensely proud of our family. This is the last of our eight children to come into this holy house for temple marriage. They, with their companions are here to participate in the marriage of this, the youngest. This is our supremely happy day, with all of our eight children married properly. They are faithful to the Lord in church service and the older ones are already rearing families in righteousness."

President Kimball looked at his calloused hands, his rough exterior and said to himself, "Here is a real son of God fulfilling his destiny."

"Success?" he said, as he grasped his hand. "That is the greatest success story I have heard. You may have accumulated millions in stocks and bonds, bank accounts, lands, industries, and still be quite a failure. You are fulfilling the purpose for which you have been sent into this world by keeping your own lives righteous, bearing and rearing this great posterity, and training them in faith and works. Why, my dear folks, you are eminently successful. God bless you."

As President Kimball finished telling his story he looked up at the portrait artist. He stood motionless in deep thought, so President Kimball said, "Yes, my brother, I have had many glimpses of heaven." The artist got the expression he sought for on President Kimball's face and was able to portray in the painting the spiritual depth of this great prophet. (Spencer W. Kimball, *Faith Precedes the Miracle*, pp. 259–61, 265.)

I too had a glimpse of heaven recently. I had been invited to seal a young couple from British Columbia in the Seattle Temple. We came together in one of the beautiful sealing rooms. For ten to twelve minutes I gave counsel to the bride and groom concerning some of the pitfalls and some of the joys and opportunities of marriage. Then I invited the groom to escort his bride to the far side of the altar, where she was to kneel, and asked him to kneel opposite her. As the bride walked to her place at the altar, I noticed that she was wearing a stunning white satin wedding dress covered with lace. It had a long, exquisite train. As she knelt at the altar she was radiant, confident, clean, sweet, and pure. The groom took his place at the altar and was equally impressive in a masculine way. I was ready to begin the ceremony when the bride's mother stood up, walked around the end of the altar, got down on her hands and knees, and began to straighten the train. First it was the satin cloth. Every wrinkle had to be straightened out. Then it was the lace. Again every wrinkle was to be smoothed out. Everything had to be perfect. It was the last finishing touch that a loving and caring and concerned mother could give to her daughter before she left to begin her own family. No peacock ever had a more beautiful train than this lovely bride had that day.

It took the mother three to four minutes to satisfy herself that everything was perfect. All the time I never took my eyes from her. As she returned around the end of the altar to her seat I followed her with my eyes. Not a word had been spoken—not even a whisper. She sat down. I continued to look at her until she raised her head. It was evident that she had been completely oblivious of others in the room. Her entire concentration was on her ravishingly beautiful daughter. Instead of a look of embarrassment on her face there was a radiance of righteous pride—not for the dress on which she had been working for months, which was beautiful beyond description, but for the daughter whom she had been molding with loving care for the previous twenty years. A mother's love could not have been more beautifully portrayed. I choked and said, "This is the most beautiful sight I have ever seen," which indeed it was.

We proceeded with the marriage and sealed the bride and groom as husband and wife for time and all eternity. The room was filled with the Holy Spirit and the guests sniffled and shed tears of joy. Indeed I had a glimpse of heaven that day.

SEOUL KOREA TEMPLE

Our hearts are filled with gratitude for this long-awaited day. This is the first such house of the Lord ever constructed on the mainland of Asia, this vast continent where dwell more than a billion of thy sons and daughters, and where through the generations of the past have lived unnumbered hosts whose lives have not been touched by the saving principles of the gospel.

Thou hast smiled with favor upon thy work here. The government of this nation has been hospitable to thy servants. Now, crowning all, is this beautiful edifice in which we meet and which we dedicate to thee.

May it ever be a house of peace, and a sanctuary from the noise and evil of the world.

◆

From the dedicatory prayer by
Gordon B. Hinckley
December 14–15, 1985

39

To Bring Out the Prisoners
from the Prison

◆

The temple in Taiwan was dedicated November 17 and 18, 1984. Five dedicatory sessions were held, conducted by President Gordon B. Hinckley of the First Presidency. In earlier times President Hinckley had supervised Church activities in the Far East for eleven years. His excitement was evident as he related experiences concerning the growth of the Church in Taiwan. Twenty years before, when he had first visited this country, there had been only a few families that were members of the Church. Now there were sufficient to sustain a temple of the Lord.

It is significant that the land on which the temple is built is a site where a prison previously stood. This is a country where land use is so intensive that it is unusual to locate a five-acre plot in such a crowded area. Initially, the land was purchased for building a chapel. One would have had to be insightful to anticipate the construction of a temple on the unused portion of the lot. It is interesting to note that where a prison to incarcerate prisoners once stood, now stands a temple that is used to release from bondage those in prison in the spirit world.

This Taipei temple is a major milestone in the fulfillment of biblical and modern-day prophecy. We are reminded of the words of Isaiah referring to the Savior's visit to the world of spirits, which occurred between the time of his crucifixion and resurrection: "I the Lord have called thee in righteousness . . . to open the blind eyes, to bring out the prisoners from the prison, and them that sit in darkness out of the prison house" (Isaiah 42:6–7) and "He hath sent me . . . to proclaim liberty to the captives, and the opening of the prison to them that are bound." (Isaiah 61:1.)

Vicarious ordinances received in the temples of the Lord by proxy for those who have died make it possible for our ancestors to be released from their spirit prison. The necessary ordinances for salvation in the kingdom of God are performed vicariously here, while those in the spirit world are being taught the gospel. "For for this cause was the gospel preached also to them that are dead, that they might be judged according to men in the flesh, but live according to God in the spirit." (1 Peter 4:6.)

The dedication of this temple represents the first time that the fulness of the gospel of Jesus Christ has been available to the Chinese in their own lands. Nearly four thousand years ago the Lord covenanted with Abraham, "Thou shalt be a blessing unto thy seed after thee, that in their hands they shall bear this ministry and Priesthood unto all nations." (Abraham 2:9.)

In the oath and covenant of the priesthood the Lord identified those who receive the priesthood and magnify their callings as the seed of Abraham. (D&C 84:33–41.) The faithful members of the Church today are the seed of Abraham either by direct lineage or by adoption. Our sons and daughters and even some of the oldsters in this dispensation are taking this ministry and priesthood unto the nations of the world. To give the fulness of the priesthood to the nations of the world, temples must be built, for the fulness of the priesthood can only be received in a house of the Lord. Thus we are now in the process of fulfilling promises made to Father Abraham by the Lord in the Abrahamic Covenant to which prophets of God have made reference in the pages of ecclesiastical history.

Temples have been constructed in many lands where sufficient numbers of members reside to sustain a temple. Latter-day prophets have stated that we will one day have hundreds of temples operating to accomplish the work to be done for the living and the dead. It is likely that we can anticipate temples will be built wherever membership justifies them.

Temples are built for a twofold purpose: (1) to redeem the dead, who have not had the opportunity in life to hear the gospel; and (2) to exalt the living, for the temple is a stepping-stone to exaltation in the celestial kingdom. The two purposes complement one another. The living make it possible for the dead to be exalted and the dead make it possible for the living to be exalted, as explained in the scriptures, for "they without us cannot be made perfect—neither can we without our dead be made perfect." (D&C 128:15.) Members of the Church should better understand this principle. It is not the will of the Lord that the temple service be performed by a few of the Saints for the many who are waiting in the spirit world. Every worthy adult member should be involved in temple service by coming to the temple regularly.

Our objective in gospel teaching and activities should be to prepare the individual to enter the presence of the Lord. Our first step in doing so is to develop an understanding of gospel principles by study and by conforming our lives to those principles. When sufficiently spiritually mature, we come to the temple to receive greater spiritual strength and to be taught by the Holy Spirit. This also enables us to perform sacred merciful service for others who have passed beyond, who are unable to do it for themselves. Thus we move into a higher realm of participation to qualify for and receive celestial glory. This is what is meant by turning the hearts of the children to the fathers and the hearts of the fathers to the children. ''For it is necessary in the ushering in of the dispensation of the fulness of times . . . that a whole and complete and perfect union, and welding together of dispensations, and keys, and powers, and glories should take place.'' (D&C 128:18.) This welding—this union—this uniting can only take place as the Saints—not just a few—but many Saints become involved on a regular basis in temple service so that many members, each contributing a little, may accomplish much, that our hearts may turn to our progenitors and that their hearts may be turned to us through all the keys, authority, priesthood, care, concern, love, and organization with which the Lord has endowed us.

This is not alone for the Zion of the West nor the Zion established by the Saints of Taiwan, but for the Zion of the world—wherever the pure in heart dwell. This work of redeeming the dead and building each other through temple service is for all the Church in various lands throughout the world. This is the redemption of Zion.

LIMA PERU TEMPLE

We thank thee for thy smiles of favor upon the people of this land, and . . . upon the many who have accepted the restored gospel. . . .

We are particularly mindful this day of the sons and daughters of Lehi. They have known so much of suffering and sorrow in their many generations. They have walked in darkness and in servitude. Now thou hast touched them by the light of the everlasting gospel. The shackles of darkness are falling from their eyes as they embrace the truths of thy great work.

◆

From the dedicatory prayer by
Gordon B. Hinckley
January 10–12, 1986

40

A One-Way Ticket Back Home

◆

My most valued treasures stored away are not stock certificates, nor bonds nor property deeds, but are the records of my ancestors. Our family searched for information about my great-grandfather for forty years. Two years ago we finally discovered information about him in a library in Keynsham, England. Thomas Derrick, we found, was born in 1777 and married Ursula Wise, who was born in 1779.

In 1836 as she lay on her deathbed, she called my grandfather to her bedside and said, "Zach, my son, do not affiliate yourself with any religion with which you are now acquainted, but when missionaries come from America preaching on street corners about a new religion and a living prophet, join that church, for it will be the true church of God." This was one year before the Mormon missionaries landed at Liverpool, England, to introduce the news of the restoration of the gospel to the people of Europe and Great Britain. She could only have obtained this knowledge from the Holy Spirit.

My grandfather, Zacharias Wise Derrick, was born in 1814. He served two seven-year apprenticeships, one as a mechanic and the other as a foundryman. It was during his second apprenticeship that his mother counseled him about the true church of God. In 1848 one of his associates at the ironworks invited him to a meeting to hear two Mormon missionaries from America. He attended, was satisfied that this was the church of which his mother spoke, joined the Church, emigrated to America in 1851, and crossed the plains in a covered wagon. For most of the balance of his life, he used his artisanship to advantage by working on the construction of the Salt Lake Temple.

When I was a small boy, Mother often talked about her youngest brother, Orson. It was obvious that her feelings and concerns about him were poignant. These were somehow transferred to me at an early age. When a stranger would come to our back door, I would pull on Mother's apron and say, "Is this Uncle Orson, Mommy? Huh?" Her answer was always, "No."

It was not until I was in my teens that Mother explained to me about him. He was born in 1882. His father died when he was eighteen months old. He grew up without the benefit of a father's guidance. When he was seventeen years of age, a group of young men from the community went to a dance at Saltair, a popular amusement pavilion on the shores of Great Salt Lake. One of them brought a generous supply of liquor. Before the evening was over, they got inebriated and were arrested for disturbing the peace. The following morning their fathers went to the county jail, got their sons released from custody, put their arms around them, and in most cases built them into pillars of the community.

On that same morning, unknown to my grandmother, two relatives went to the jail, arranged for Uncle Orson's release, told him he had disgraced the family, bought him a one-way ticket to the Northwest, and told him never to return. He was obedient to their instruction. Mother told me that on several occasions she heard Grandmother crying in the night. She went to her bedside, and Grandma would sob, "I wonder where my wandering boy is tonight?" Without the help of family and Church, it was likely that in the lumber camps of the Northwest Uncle Orson's life-style was such that he did not take advantage of his heritage.

In his revelation about the spirit world, Joseph F. Smith told about those spirits who had been faithful in the testimony of Jesus while in the flesh, but did not have the opportunity of receiving a knowledge of the gospel in mortality. They must receive those ordinances vicariously. He told about the unrepentant who had defiled themselves while in the flesh. Those would be taught gospel principles in the spirit world and would have an opportunity of repentance and redemption through obedience to the ordinances of the gospel. (See D&C 138:57–59.)

We have good reason to believe that Ursula Wise Derrick would qualify for entrance into the celestial kingdom. Family members have received temple blessings in her behalf and in behalf of her husband that will enable them to receive whatever reward they are entitled to by virtue of their works.

We do not know much about Uncle Orson. We do know he did not have the same opportunity that most of his friends had during his adolescent years. We also know that God is a just god and that justice will prevail. We are neither the judge nor the jury. Therefore, we must perform the temple ordinances by proxy for Uncle Orson to ensure that if he qualifies, those sacred blessings will await his claim. When the proof of a person's death is not available, one hundred and ten years must elapse from his birth to ensure that he is deceased before his temple blessings can be administered by proxy.

Even though I have never seen Uncle Orson I have gained a great love for him. I would so much like to purchase him a one-way ticket back home—back to his Father in Heaven where he can dwell with his forever family in the tranquility of celestial glory. I know I can't do this for him, but I can ensure that his temple blessings are available for him in 1992 so that he can receive a reward according to his works—whatever reward that might be.

It is probable that every family has an Ursula Wise Derrick and every family has an Uncle Orson in their family lines. It is the family's responsibility to locate the genealogical data that will uniquely identify them and arrange for their passage back to their heavenly abode so that they too might be able to claim their reward according to their works.

BUENOS AIRES ARGENTINA TEMPLE

Particularly do we thank thee, our Father, for the faithful missionaries who have served, and continue now to labor, in this and surrounding lands, who teach thy truths and who lead thy children by thy everlasting light. We remember that it was in this very city of Buenos Aires, on Christmas Day in the year 1925, just sixty years ago, that Elder Melvin J. Ballard, an Apostle of the Lord, dedicated all of South America for the preaching of the gospel. What a fulfillment to an inspired prayer!

◆

From the dedicatory prayer by
Thomas S. Monson
January 17–19, 1986

41

The Turning of Hearts

◆

On April 3, 1836, a marvelous manifestation took place in the temple in Kirtland, Ohio. Behind a veil which had been dropped to segregate the pulpit area from the large temple room, Joseph Smith and Oliver Cowdery bowed in silent prayer and supplicated their Father in Heaven. When they arose, the Lord Jesus Christ appeared to them standing on the breastwork of the pulpit. The description of his visit is one of the most colorful and sacred events to be found in the scriptures. (See D&C 110:1–4.) Following this manifestation other heavenly messengers appeared, including Elijah the prophet, who stood before them and said: "Behold, the time has fully come, which was spoken of by the mouth of Malachi—testifying that he (Elijah) should be sent, before the great and dreadful day of the Lord come—to turn the hearts of the fathers to the children, and the children to the fathers, lest the whole earth be smitten with a curse." (D&C 110:14–15.)

To turn one's heart toward another is to become concerned about the other's welfare and those principles and powers and blessings that affect his welfare. In particular, we are concerned about the eternal welfare of our extended family. Wife must be sealed to husband and children to parents as far back as we can trace our family genealogy. "If it were not so, the whole earth would be utterly wasted at his coming" (D&C 2:3), for the plan of salvation would otherwise be frustrated. When we seal one person to another, we must first properly identify each individual. Have you ever considered how many Joseph Smiths or Mary Browns or John Taylors might have lived since the time of Adam? Before one person is sealed to another, each must be uniquely identified. There may be many John Taylors, but only one John Taylor was born on a particular day, died on a particular day, married a woman with a particular name who was born on a particular day, and so forth. The gathering of such information to uniquely identify an individual is known as genealogical research. To accomplish this work a charge has been given to each family and individual by the Lord.

The Genealogical Society of Utah, which was organized in 1894, microfilms name data records throughout the world. The book *Roots* written by Alex Haley has stirred the interest of the world during the past decade in gathering family genealogy and has been a contributing factor in creating a greater interest in genealogical research.

In 1980 a World Conference on Records was held in Salt Lake City, sponsored by the Genealogical Society of Utah, an arm of The Church of Jesus Christ of Latter-day Saints. Twelve thousand people from throughout the world were in attendance at the opening session of a four-day conference. On that occasion, Salt Lake City won for itself the reputation of being the genealogical center of the world.

In October 1985 a new four-story, 120,000-square-foot modern library, committed solely to genealogical research, was dedicated. It has attracted the attention of genealogists, archivists, scholars, and researchers from throughout the world. Progress is being made therein in utilizing the most modern technology available to store and access the vast amount of information that is being gathered. A study was made several years ago by those affiliated with the Genealogical Society of Utah assigned to name acquisition. They roughly estimate that data is extant throughout the world on approximately six billion names of people who were born prior to A.D. 1900. Add to that the name data on those who have been born since that time and one gets an idea of the enormity of the collection and storage assignment in connection with Malachi's prophecy for which we will be held responsible as the hearts of the children turn to their fathers.

> From about 1000 A.D. Chinese and Korean clans have kept records of their ancestors as part of their family duties. . . . In the twenty-fourth session of Trent, held in November 1563, the Council required that parish registers be kept of marriages and baptisms throughout all the Catholic world—Europe, the British Isles, and colonies in the New World and India. Protestant churches continued this registration even after breaking off from the Catholic Church, creating a great treasury of records from which information for temple ordinances can be drawn. . . . By the end of the sixteenth century, many European countries and their colonies were keeping censuses, records of civil transactions, and immigration records. . . . The *Code Civil des Français* was

adopted March 21, 1804, in Napoleonic Europe—the basis for how vital statistics are registered in much of the world today. (Jimmy B. Parker, "I Have a Question," *Ensign*, January 1977, p. 72.)

A search has proven futile for any private societies or organizations existing for the purpose of gathering and storing records for the dead prior to Elijah's visit to Joseph Smith and Oliver Cowdery in 1836. "In 1844, the New England Historic and Genealogical Society was formed to gather genealogical records. Slowly, more such groups were organized until 200 were in existence in the United States alone by 1966." (Ibid.) Within the next ten years that number skyrocketed to eight hundred and has continued to increase until, according to *Time* magazine, it has become the third most popular hobby in the United States, exceeded only by stamp and coin collecting. The turning of the hearts of the children and the fathers to one another is becoming more evident every year, which is fulfilling the propecy made by Malachi nearly three thousand years ago relating to this dispensation of time.

DENVER COLORADO TEMPLE

We thank thee for the restoration of thine everlasting priesthood, including the keys to bind in heaven that which is bound on earth, which keys will be exercised in this thy holy temple.

Touch the hearts of thy people that they may look to this temple as a refuge from the evil and turmoil of the world. May they ever live worthy of the blessings here to be found. May they be prompted to seek the records of their forbears and to serve here in their behalf, under the plan which thou hast revealed for the salvation and exaltation of thy children of all generations.

◆

From the dedicatory prayer by
Ezra Taft Benson
October 24, 1986

42

Preparing a Record
Worthy of All Acceptation

◆

Since the beginning of time the Lord has counseled his children to record their genealogy. Adam kept a "book of the generations of Adam" in which was recorded the genealogy "of the children of God." (Moses 6:8.) Abraham's posterity recorded their genealogy sufficiently well that they were able to reconstruct family relationships when they returned from exile in Babylon. (See Ezra 2 and 10.) The Jews at the time of Christ were genealogy conscious. Considerable space has been devoted in the scriptures to record family relationships. Genealogies are important to the fulfillment of the plan of salvation. Genealogy, temples, and the Melchizedek Priesthood are so closely allied that they are reliant upon one another in God's blueprint for man's destiny.

Brigham Young explained that the main purpose of the Melchizedek Priesthood is to seal families until the chain of generations is made perfect from the latest generation back to Father Adam. (See *JD* 13:280.) Children born to parents who have been sealed together in the bonds of holy matrimony in the temple for time and for all eternity are automatically sealed to their parents. We say they are born in the covenant. A wife must be sealed to her husband, and children not born in the covenant must be sealed to their parents—not only the living, but also the dead (by proxy) to perfect their chain of generations. The sealing of families cannot be accomplished unless the dead are first uniquely identified. This requires genealogical research in behalf of our own kindred dead.

In 1894 Wilford Woodruff said, "We want the Latter-day Saints from this time to trace their genealogies as far as they can, and to be sealed to their fathers and mothers. Have children sealed to their parents, and run this chain through as far as you can get it. . . . This is the will of the Lord to this people." (*MS* 56:339.) In 1899 President Lorenzo Snow said, "This entire continent is the land of

Zion, and the time will come when there will be Temples established over every portion of the land, and we will go into these
Temples and work for our kindred dead night and day, that the
work of the Lord may be speedily accomplished, that Jesus may
come and present the kingdom to his Father.'' (*MS* 61:546.)

"Others are operating with us, I mean all the men of God who
ever lived, and they are as much interested as we are, and a good
deal more, for they know more, and 'they without us cannot be
made perfect' neither can we be perfected without them.'' (John
Taylor, *JD* 17:213.) "This work of administering the ordinances of
the house of God to the dead . . . will require the whole of the Millennium, with Jesus at the head of the resurrected dead to attend
to it.'' (Wilford Woodruff, *JD* 13:327.)

> President Brigham Young has said that during the Millennium
> those on the other side will work hand in hand with those in mortal-
> ity and will furnish the names of the dead which we are unable to
> obtain through our research, and thus every soul that is entitled to
> these blessings shall be ferreted out and his work done for him. I fully
> believe that many among the dead, those who are worthy, are even
> now engaged in compiling records and arranging information, if it has
> not already been done, for this very purpose. Why should they not be
> so engaged? (Joseph Fielding Smith, "Salvation for the Living and the
> Dead," *Relief Society Magazine* 5:678.)

"When you have done all you can do and have reached the
limit, what will happen? As always in the past, man's extremity is
God's opportunity. The Lord never helps us where we can help
ourselves. This is our day. We don't expect Him to do miraculous
things that we can do for ourselves. When we have done our utmost,
then will come God's opportunity.'' (*Melvin J. Ballard, Crusader for
Righteousness*, p. 253.)

The operation of temples relied solely upon family research until
1962. By that time family research could not meet the demands of
the temples, so President David O. McKay approved the in-house
(Genealogical Department) extraction of names from microfilm
records. This continued until 1978 when the stake name extraction
program was introduced, shifting the responsibility of extracting
names from the genealogical department to the priesthood in the
stakes of the Church. The whole system is moving toward decen-
tralization from Church headquarters to the stakes so that each temple district can satisfy its own temple needs. Deceased persons identified from microfilm records whose names are processed through

name extraction will eventually, through family research, be tied into their family lines. The processing of their name data to enable their temple work to be performed will expand the International Genealogical Index (IGI). This expanded index will increasingly enhance the effectiveness of genealogical research.

In an attempt to obtain more family data and to improve the quality and accuracy of the Family File, families of the Church were requested to submit a more accurate and up-to-date four-generation record. The response was most gratifying. In 1981 long-range plans were approved to bring twenty-first century technology into the storage, processing, and accessing of name data. Much has since been accomplished in doing so and progress is continuing.

Some members have the misunderstanding that the computer will assimilate information obtained from the microfilming of records and name extraction and produce family group records and pedigree charts on family lines of Church members. The computer will serve as a valuable tool in genealogical research, but is incapable of replacing family research. The responsibility of each family is to research back as far as possible to uniquely identify each ancestor. This will enable the dead to be saved—and us too. "Let us, therefore, as a church and a people, and as Latter-day Saints, offer unto the Lord an offering in righteousness; and let us present in his holy temple, when it is finished, a book containing the records of our dead, which shall be worthy of all acceptation." (D&C 128:24.)

FREIBERG DDR TEMPLE

On this day of dedication our hearts turn to
thee. We thank thee for this holy temple in
this land and nation. We thank thee for all who
have made possible its buildings—the officers
of the government who have given encourage-
ment and made available land and materials,
the architects and the builders, and all who
have made possible this glorious day of dedication.

◆

From the dedicatory prayer by
Gordon B. Hinckley
June 29–30, 1985

35

Royalty and Temple Marriage

◆

Many are familiar with the beautiful story of Cinderella. It has kindled in the hearts and minds of little girls dreams and aspirations that have smoldered through their adolescence. Nearly every young lady has dreamed of marrying a prince, but has soon thereafter placed doing so beyond the realms of reality.

The Apostle Peter, writing to the Saints of his day who held the Melchizedek Priesthood, addressed them as "a royal priesthood." (1 Peter 2:9.) Why should he make such a salutation? The traditional attribute of royalty is the royal blood line.

> In general, the Lord sends to earth in the lineage of Jacob those spirits who in pre-existence developed an especial talent for spirituality and for recognizing truth. Those born in this lineage [have] the blood of Israel in their veins and [find] it easy to accept the gospel. . . .
>
> Since much of Israel has been scattered among the Gentile nations, it follows that millions of people have mixed blood, blood that is part Israel and part Gentile. The more of the blood of Israel that an individual has, the easier it is for him to believe the message of salvation as taught by the authorized agents of the Lord. This principle . . . the Lord had in mind when he said to certain Jews: "I am the good shepherd, and know my sheep, and am known of mine. . . . But ye believe not, because ye are not of my sheep. . . . My sheep hear my voice, and I know them, and they follow me." (John 10:14, 26–27.) (Bruce R. McConkie, *Mormon Doctrine*, p. 81.)

The royal line of Israel is through the lineage of Abraham, Isaac, and Jacob. Nevertheless, one can enjoy all the promises and special blessings the Lord has given to the children of Israel through adoption into the house of Israel. Regardless of their blood line, all those who receive the gospel and obey the principles of the gospel are adopted into the lineage of Abraham. (See Abraham 2:9–11.) "The effect of the Holy Ghost upon a Gentile, is to purge out the old blood, and make him actually of the seed of Abraham." (*Teachings of the Prophet Joseph Smith*, p. 150.) In the oath and covenant of the priesthood we learn that "whoso is faithful unto the obtaining these two priesthoods of which I have spoken, and the magnifying their calling, are sanctified by the Spirit unto the renewing of their bodies. They become the sons of Moses and of Aaron and the seed of Abraham, and the church and kingdom, and the elect of God." (D&C 84:33-34.) To be the seed of Abraham means to be of his lineage. Therefore, all the promises that have been given to Abraham and his posterity are given to them, predicated upon their righteousness, as though they had been of his actual blood lineage.

Royalty connotes that there is a king and a kingdom. In temple marriages Heavenly Father is the king. The kingdom is the kingdom of God. The groom is the prince and the bride is the princess. The prince has royal blood. He inherits or rather shares his father's kingdom. "Therefore all that [his] Father hath shall be given unto him," the Savior promised. (D&C 84:38.) The princess shares the kingdom as well, for "neither is the man without the woman, neither the woman without the man, in the Lord." (1 Corinthians 11:11.)

In the sealing room of the temple a beautiful princess kneels on one side of the altar and a handsome prince on the other. He who is authorized seals the couple in holy matrimony—not until death parts them, but for time and for all eternity, for he holds the authority to bind in heaven that which is bound on earth, or to seal in heaven that which is sealed on earth, and to record in heaven that which is recorded on earth.

This is the same authority to which the Savior referred when he said to Peter, "I will give unto thee the keys of the kingdom of heaven: and whatsoever thou shalt bind on earth shall be bound in heaven." (Matthew 16:19.) These same keys were given by Elijah the prophet to Joseph Smith and Oliver Cowdery in the Kirtland Temple on April 3, 1836. The power to seal is exercised by one given the authority to bind in holy matrimony by God's and man's requirements. Thus having satisfied civil and eternal law, a new family begins in mortality to be extended into the eternities based upon their remaining faithful to the covenants they receive in the temple.

That evening the two will kneel down at their bedside and offer a prayer of thanksgiving and blessing to their Father in Heaven. As they do so they will begin to share the innermost desires of their hearts, their hopes, their dreams, and their ambitions. An arc will be struck that will begin the process of welding them together as one. As they give of themselves to one another, their lives mold together until they can say of their marriage, "Man is not without the woman nor the woman without the man in the Lord."

It now behooves the young prince to build his wife into a beautiful queen and the princess to build her husband into a great king, for no marriage can be left in the hands of circumstance. The couple must control their destiny by working, planning, and living in harmony with gospel principles. As they do so, the Holy Spirit will ratify their sacred union. The bride's childhood fantasy of Prince Charming thus becomes reality—which is only the beginning.

STOCKHOLM SWEDEN TEMPLE

Bless this nation where is found thy temple, and its sister
nations. . . .

Save these nations from war and oppression, and may their people
look to thee and open their doors and hearts to thy messengers of
eternal truth. Tens of thousands have walked reverently through
this sacred structure. May the impressions of their visits stir within
them a desire to learn more of thee and thy purposes with reference to thy children. May they seek and find and learn.

◆

From the dedicatory prayer by
Gordon B. Hinckley
July 2–4, 1985

36

The Holy Spirit of Promise

◆

Some people think that because they have been baptized they are guaranteed entrance into the celestial kingdom of God. Others assume that because they have received their temple blessings they qualify for eternal life, which is life with our Eternal Father or exaltation. However, the sanctity of the kingdom of God is protected by the Holy Spirit of Promise, which is the "name-title . . . used in connection with the sealing and ratifying power of the Holy Ghost." (Bruce R. McConkie, *Mormon Doctrine*, p. 361.)

The Lord said, "All covenants, contracts, bonds, obligations, oaths, vows, performances, connections, associations, or expectations, that are not made and entered into and sealed by the Holy Spirit of promise . . . are of no efficacy, virtue, or force in and after the resurrection from the dead; for all contracts that are not made unto this end have an end when men are dead." (D&C 132:7.) Thus every ordinance pertaining to the kingdom of God, whether in the temple of the Lord or out of the temple, must be sealed or ratified by the Holy Spirit of Promise to be effective.

An unworthy candidate for baptism might deceive the elders and get the ordinance performed, but no one can lie to the Holy Ghost and get by undetected. Accordingly, the baptism of an unworthy and unrepentant person would not be sealed by the Spirit; it would not be ratified by the Holy Ghost; the unworthy person would not be justified by the Spirit in his actions. If thereafter he became worthy through repentance and obedience, the seal would then be put in force. Similarly, if a worthy person is baptized, with the ratifying approval of the Holy Ghost attending the performance, yet the seal may be broken by subsequent sin.

These principles also apply to every other ordinance and performance in the Church. Thus if both parties are "just and true," if they are worthy, a ratifying seal is placed on their temple marriage; if they are unworthy, they are not justified by the Spirit and the ratification of the Holy Ghost is withheld. Subsequent worthiness will put the seal in force and unrighteousness will break any seal. (McConkie, *Mormon Doctrine*, p. 362.)

Ratification of ordinances we have received comes through righteous living. At the conclusion of the chapter that contains the Beatitudes in the New Testament, the Savior said, "Be ye therefore perfect, even as your Father which is in heaven is perfect." (Matthew 5:48.) The chapter preceding this verse contains instructions on how one might become more nearly perfect. As noted, the Beatitudes themselves represent a formula as to how one might better strive for perfection.

The Lord said, "Seek ye earnestly the best gifts, . . . for verily I say unto you, they are given for the benefit of those who love me and keep all my commandments, *and him that seeketh so to do; that all may be benefited that seek or that ask of me*, that ask and not for a sign that they may consume it upon their lusts." (D&C 46:8, 9; italics added.) The Lord does not expect us to be perfect now, but he does expect us to strive continually to become perfect. If we continue to strive with real intent, not walking in our own way but striving in accord with his words as spoken by the mouths of his holy prophets, the reward will come.

Perfection is the eternal objective. It is not impossible. It comes by living each hour of each day perfectly. Perfection is the by-product of striving, and striving is the result of committing ourselves to do what we should do when we should do it. To know what we should do requires study and learning and doing the things of God. As we do so we gain understanding.

Men by nature are carnal, sensual, and devilish. Unless they put forth effort otherwise, they remain in that state. Mortality is a probationary state where man might prove himself and prepare for his eternal destiny. Mortality is a testing ground through the exercise of agency. We are given all that the Lord sees fit for us to receive and are tested according to that knowledge. Whether we choose to be obedient to what we receive or to be disobedient, we will be rewarded accordingly.

As we exercise our agency, we sometimes commit sin. If we are not sorry for sin we have committed and have no desire to repent and improve, we will be held responsible to satisfy the demands of eternal justice. If we are sorry for sin we have committed, we can repent and be forgiven, in which case the demands of eternal justice will be satisfied by the atoning sacrifice of Jesus Christ wherein he suffered at Gethsemane and gave his life in agony on Calvary.

The steps of repentance are (1) recognition, (2) remorse, (3) restitution, and (4) resolve. If our desire is for good, we can gain help from the Lord through prayer and study. The Lord blesses us in accordance with our desires and actions.

The Savior said: "This is eternal lives—to know the only wise and true God, and Jesus Christ, whom he hath sent. I am he. Receive ye, therefore, my law." (D&C 132:24.) The temple is available to assist us in our quest for perfection and for the ratifying seal of the Holy Spirit of Promise. Having received our endowments, if we are faithful to the covenants we have made with the Lord in the temple, if we search the scriptures regularly to better understand the gospel of Jesus Christ, and if we return to the temple often, we will draw near unto the Lord and he will draw near unto us. We will come to know God through a better understanding of him and his purpose and his ways. This is how we can become "sanctified from all sin, and enjoy the words of eternal life in this world, and eternal life in the world to come, even immortal glory." (Moses 6:59.) This is how we can ensure that the priesthood ordinances we receive will be sealed by the Holy Spirit of Promise.

CHICAGO ILLINOIS TEMPLE

We are mindful that thy Prophet Joseph Smith, and his brother Hyrum, were martyred in Carthage, Illinois, at a time of terrible conflict and persecution. May there now be peace and good will in the land. Bless the officers of this state and nation that they shall stand firmly for those principles of freedom and equity which were written into the Constitution of the United States under thine inspiration.

◆

From the dedicatory prayer by
Gordon B. Hinckley
August 9–13, 1985

37
Blessings of Temple Service

◆

Temples of the Lord are a resource to be used by faithful members to spiritually enrich and ennoble their lives and the lives of their immediate and extended family members. When members of the Church attend the temple regularly, inner peace calms the soul; the Spirit of the Lord permeates the home; love and respect deepen between family members; problems are more clearly defined; solutions are more apparent; emotions are more serene in family relations; divorces significantly decrease in the Church community; lives of participants and their associates are spiritually enriched; and children are more likely to socialize with good friends, be more communicative with parents, attend seminary and institute, serve missions, be active in the Church, better understand gospel principles, and qualify for a forever family relationship.

These blessings are more certain when parents set a good example in and out of the home, hold family home evenings regularly, and pray together regularly as a family. Attending the temple regularly develops a commitment and a dedication to maintain such discipline in the home.

This is why one bishop could say that

> he concentrated on getting his people into the temple and as a result in five years he had not had an interview with any members of his ward concerning serious family problems. In five years there had been no divorces in his ward, 95 percent of his people had been married in the temple, and nearly every young man and many young women had gone to serve missions.
>
> Another bishop said, "I am by nature a lazy bishop. I do not care to struggle with the troubles that affect the members of my ward adversely, so I take them to the temple. When I do this I find they pay their tithing, hold their family home evenings, and they teach themselves the commandments and principles of the Lord's kingdom. Welfare problems are minimal." (W. Grant Bangerter, First Quorum of the Seventy Meeting Address, 5 February 1986.)

An outstanding stake president said, "It is my feeling that the temple is both the key to activation plus the key to retaining those activated." During the past nine years 344 prospective elders have been activated in his stake, the percentage of adult men holding the Melchizedek Priesthood has increased from 60 to 70, the average attendance at sacrament meeting has increased from 43 to 56 percent; and the Melchizedek Priesthood attendance at priesthood meeting has increased from 55 to 67 percent.

The activation of prospective elders in his stake has affected the lives of more than eleven hundred immediate family members. These former prospective elders have joined other stake members in building their family spirituality by coming to the temple regularly, which has resulted in their stake's becoming an example in temple worship.

"Those who enter the temples and desire to obtain most from the experience must seek to purify their hearts in preparation. Only those who do so share fully in the blessings that flow from the temple." (John A. Widtsoe, "The House of the Lord," *Improvement Era*, April 1936, p. 228.) Thus one should prepare himself to come to the temple. If an endowed member will remain faithful to the covenants he has made with the Lord in the temple, if he will study the scriptures regularly, and if he will return to the temple regularly, his mind will be enlightened and his understanding quickened so as to better understand the truths of eternity.

In the temple, when properly prepared, a person is taught by the Holy Spirit. Why is it necessary to study in preparation? The prophet Alma said that by nature men are carnal, sensual, and devilish. (Alma 42:10.) If one comes to the temple with carnal thoughts he cannot be taught by the Holy Spirit, for nothing unclean can enter the presence of the Lord. It is possible to eliminate carnal thoughts by replacing them with spiritual thoughts that can best be attained through prayer and by studying the scriptures. Together with sincere prayer and faithful living, we are prepared for true temple worship where we are taught from on high.

The Lord said, "For this is the covenant that I will make with the house of Israel. . . . I will put my laws into their mind, and write them in their hearts: and I will be to them a God, and they shall be to me a people." (Hebrews 8:10.) The Holy Spirit not only teaches knowledge in the temple but inculcates into the soul of man character traits such as love, devotion, commitment, charity, faith, hope, virtue, temperance, patience, brotherly kindness, godliness, humility, diligence, long-suffering, gentleness, and meekness. If this were not so, how could temples of the Lord be staffed by thousands of ordinance workers from varied backgrounds who serve without monetary remuneration, and how could the temples be attended by hundreds of thousands of patrons each month in a spiritual atmosphere that rises above and beyond earthly relationships? In the temple each day scores of participants voluntarily express their happiness and deep appreciation for the opportunity of serving in the house of the Lord. "To a careful observer, doubtful as to the value of temple work, the abundant evidences of spiritual growth of those who engage in it is most convincing. There is a calm and sweet serenity about them which is indeed heavenly." (George F. Richards, "Latter-day Temples," *Improvement Era*, May 1930, p. 471.)

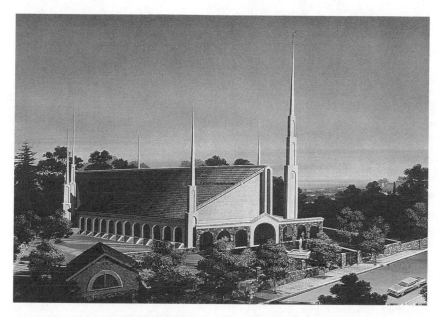

JOHANNESBURG SOUTH AFRICA TEMPLE

Almighty God, wilt thou overrule for the blessing and safety of thy faithful Saints. We pray for peace in this troubled land. Bless this nation which has befriended thy servants. May those who rule in the offices of the government be inspired to find a basis for reconciliation among those who now are in conflict one with another. May the presence of thy house on the soil of this land bring blessings to the entire nation.

May guardian angels stand watch over this holy house we humbly ask thee. May it be preserved from destruction or defilement. May it be a place of holiness, a haven of peace, a sanctuary from the storms of life.

From the dedicatory prayer by
Gordon B. Hinckley
August 24–25, 1985

38

Return and Feast at the
Table of the Lord

◆

Some members of the Church are disappointed when coming to the temple for the first time because the endowment was not what they expected; some are disappointed because nothing dramatic occurred during their visit; and some are offended because everything did not conform to the styles and culture of the society with which they are familiar. As a consequence they do not return to take advantage of what they can do for their progenitors and to enrich their lives through temple blessings.

Obviously, they either are unprepared to understand or do not listen to the remarkable promises made to those who are faithful. One must realize that the temple endowment was first given to Adam. If the same measuring rule applies to the judgment of all of God's children, the measuring device should not vary from basic standards.

In the Book of Mormon we read of King Benjamin, who in his old age called his people to the temple and, as an introduction to his message, said, "Open your ears that ye may hear, and your hearts that ye may understand, and your minds that the mysteries of God may be unfolded to your view." (Mosiah 2:9.) Today we reiterate that same counsel to those who come to the temple that each may listen, understand, and learn.

Preparatory to worshipping in the temple, one must realize that the sacred temple ordinances are symbolic of deep spiritual truths. Symbolism should not bother us. We live in a world of symbols— the alphabet, our monetary system, road signs, etc. Each is much more meaningful than what one perceives by the eye. And so it is with the ordinances of the temple; they have deep spiritual meaning that we should strive to understand. To fully understand the significance of the sacred ordinances is a lifelong quest.

The temple endowment encompasses the temple ordinances. In spite of our best efforts to learn, we will probably gain more understanding of the endowment in the next life than in mortality. As our understanding of the endowment expands, so increases our spirituality and our knowledge of God's plan of salvation for his children, which plan is the gospel of Jesus Christ.

To those who are willing to make the effort to prepare themselves, a visit to the temple is a wonderful experience. We prepare ourselves through study, prayer, and living in harmony with gospel teachings. We should not overlook the principle that temple attendance itself gives the individual a greater resolve to properly prepare himself for temple worship. Elder John A. Widtsoe wrote, "Temple worship implies a great effort of mind and concentration if we are to understand the mighty symbols that pass in review before us." To get the most out of temple worship "everything must be arranged to attune our hearts, our minds, and our souls to the work. Everything about us must contribute to the peace of mind that enables us to study and to understand the mysteries that unfold before us." ("Temple Service," *A Book of Remembrance Lesson Book: First Year Junior Genealogy Classes,* pp. 40–43.)

The temple is a place of revelation for those who attend and are spiritually prepared. The Holy Ghost is the revelator. Problems we have pondered and prayed about are often resolved in the temple.

> So, revelation always comes; it is not imposed upon a person; it must be drawn to us by faith, seeking and working. . . . I believe that the busy person on the farm, in the shop, in the office, or in the household, who has his worries and troubles, can solve his problems better and more quickly in the house of the Lord than anywhere else. If he will leave his problems behind and in the temple work for himself and for his dead, he will confer a mighty blessing upon those who have gone before, and quite as large a blessing will come to him, for at the most unexpected moments, in or out of the temple will come to him, as a revelation, the solution of the problems that vex his life. That is the gift that comes to those who enter the temple properly, because it is a place where revelations may be expected. (John A. Widtsoe, "Temple Worship," *Utah Genealogical and Historical Magazine* 12:63–64.)

To those who were disappointed, to those who did not understand, to those who were offended in their first visit to the temple—would you sanction your child's dropping out of first grade because it was different from what he expected? Would you countenance your child's dropping out of high school because he did not understand geometry? Would you drop out of college because the class structuring was different from that to which you were accustomed?

Come to the temple! Return and feast at the table of the Lord that you may have joy in this life and eternal glory in the life to come.

FRANKFURT GERMANY TEMPLE

Wherefore . . . feast upon the words of Christ; for behold, the words of Christ will tell you all things that ye should do.

Wherefore . . . if ye cannot understand (these words) it will be because ye ask not, neither do ye knock; wherefore, ye are not brought into the light, but must perish in the dark.

For behold, again I say unto you that if ye will enter in by the way, and receive the Holy Ghost, it will show unto you all things ye should do.

◆

2 Nephi 32:3–5

43

The Dispensation of the
Fulness of Times

◆

We are now living in the dispensation of the fulness of times. It is the dispensation of which the Lord says, "I will gather together in one all things, both which are in heaven, and which are on earth; and also with all those whom my Father hath given me out of the world." (D&C 27:13–14.) The Apostle Paul in his epistle to the Ephesian Saints wrote, "That in the dispensation of the fulness of times he [Christ] might gather in one all things . . . both which are in heaven, and which are on earth." (Ephesians 1:10.)

Joseph Smith received the following revelation: "For unto you, the Twelve . . . and the First Presidency . . . is the power of this priesthood given, for the last days and for the last time, in the which is the dispensation of the fulness of times. Which power you hold, in connection with all those who have received a dispensation at any time from the beginning of creation." (D&C 112:30–31.) "Every key, power, and authority ever dispensed from heaven to men on earth, which is necessary for their eternal salvation, has already been restored in this dispensation." (Bruce R. McConkie, *Mormon Doctrine*, p. 200.)

Joseph Smith, speaking of the dead, wrote, "For we without them cannot be made perfect. . . . Neither can they nor we be made perfect without those who have died in the gospel also; for it is necessary in the ushering in of the dispensation of the fulness of times, which dispensation is now beginning to usher in, that a whole and complete and perfect union, and welding together of dispensations, and keys, and powers, and glories should take place, and be revealed from the days of Adam even to the present time." (D&C 128:18.) "This is the great work of the last dispensation—the redemption of the living and the dead." (Wilford Woodruff, *JD* 21:194.) This can only be done in the house of the Lord.

Jehovah came to earth as the Babe of Bethlehem. Under divine instruction he was named Jesus. He grew through childhood and gained stature. "He received not of the fulness at first, but continued from grace to grace, until he received a fulness." (D&C 93:13.) He served his ministry for a short three years during which he taught the people living then—and for all generations to come. Because of his divine sonship he had the power to lay his life down and the power to take it up again. He suffered in Gethsemane and sacrificed his life. In doing so he satisfied the demands of eternal justice to atone for our sins, which required the supreme sacrifice. Only he could do so, for he was the perfect one. He is our example. We should follow in his footsteps both in deed and in destiny. He is our Savior and our Redeemer.

As we follow in his footsteps we too can become saviors of men. President Wilford Woodruff wrote:

> The Lord has raised up saviors upon Mount Zion, and the kingdom is the Lord's. It is His work. And we have the great power as Latter-day Saints to go into these Temples and redeem our dead, and attend to ordinances for them that they never heard of in their day and generation. What will be the condition of these saviors upon Mount Zion? These Saints of the Lord will hold the keys of salvation to their father's house to the endless ages of eternity. There never will be a time when that power will be taken from them. We ought to realize these things, and we ought to prize the blessings which God has put in our hands. (MS 53:405.)

But how are we to become saviors on Mount Zion? By building temples, erecting baptismal fonts, and going forth and receiving all the ordinances, baptisms, confirmations, washings, anointings, ordinations, and scaling powers upon our heads in behalf of all our progenitors who are dead, and redeem them that they may come forth in the first resurrection and be exalted to thrones of glory with them, and herein is the chain that binds the hearts of the fathers to the children, and the children to the fathers, which fulfills the mission of Elijah. (See Joseph Smith, HC 6:184.)

Wilford Woodruff said, "When the Savior comes a thousand years will be devoted to this work of redemption." (JD 19:230.) At the beginning of construction on the Salt Lake Temple, Brigham Young said:

> I want to see the Temple built in a manner that it will endure through the Millennium. This is not the only Temple we shall build;

there will be hundreds of them built and dedicated to the Lord. . . . When the Millennium is over, and all the sons and daughters of Adam and Eve, down to the last of their posterity, who come within the reach of the clemency of the Gospel, have been redeemed in hundreds of Temples through administration of their children as proxies for them, I want that Temple still to stand as a proud monument of faith, perseverance and industry of the Saints of God in the mountains, in the nineteenth century. (*JD* 10:254.)

In order to administer a deceased person's temple blessings by proxy, that person must be uniquely identified. But how can we provide temple blessings for those whom we cannot uniquely identify? Brigham Young said: "The gospel is now preached to the spirits in prison, and when the time comes for the servants of God to officiate for them, the names of those who have received the Gospel in the spirit will be revealed by the angels of God and the spirits of just men made perfect; also the place of their birth, the age in which they lived, and everything regarding them that is necessary to be recorded on earth, and they will then be saved so as to find admittance into the presence of God." (*JD* 9:317.)

And thus all these treasures that God has given in all the dispensations of time, together with his worthy children, must be welded together. And how is this to be done? It will be done as the hearts of the children turn to the fathers and the hearts of the fathers turn to the children. It is this love and concern that will fuel action to weld the dispensations into a whole and complete and perfect union. This is our responsibility, which is characterized by the baptismal fonts in our holy temples. The weight of the font and the water on the backs of the twelve oxen is symbolic of the burden of the children of Israel to bring salvation to the world; when this is accomplished, the Savior can present the kingdom to the Father, saying, "It is finished."

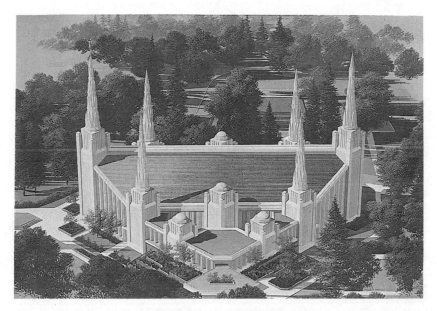

PORTLAND OREGON TEMPLE

Dear Father, we are so grateful. We thank thee for this day, for its beauty, for these woods in which we meet. They remind us of the fact that thou didst appear with thy Son to the boy Joseph Smith in woods, and that the woods were thy first temple, and in this tranquil and beautiful place we gather today with thankful hearts.

We know this work is thine. We know that it is a great work of love. We know that it is an expression of thy love for us and of the love of thy Beloved Son who gave his life for us and of our love for our brethren and sisters—our forebears—who cannot proceed under thy eternal plan without ordinances which are performed upon the earth. And, it is for this purpose that this house is to be built.

◆

Gordon B. Hinckley at ground-breaking
ceremony
September 20, 1986

44

Making Major Strides

◆

President Kimball said: "To travel listlessly is just futile. One should have a destination and a goal to reach. One should determine what he wants out of life and then bend every effort toward reaching that goal. . . . One of the basic tasks for each individual is the making of decisions. A dozen times a day we come to a fork in the road and must decide which way we will go. Some alternatives are long and hard, but they take us in the right direction toward our ultimate goal; others are short, wide, and pleasant, but they go off in the wrong direction. . . . The time to decide that we will settle for nothing less than an opportunity to live eternally with our Father is now, so that every choice we make will be affected by our determination to let nothing interfere with attaining that ultimate goal." (*The Teachings of Spencer W. Kimball*, pp. 163–65.)

There are two schools of thought in setting goals: (1) A goal set too high becomes a discouraging rather than a motivating factor. A modest goal results in one's striving to do a little better than before, which in some situations might be best. (2) But setting high goals forces creative thinking. This concept may result in failure to reach the objective, but the results will often be much more satisfactory than when one aims only for "a little better than before."

For example, when the Liverpool, England District Saints were preparing for stakehood they set a goal for themselves to increase sacrament meeting attendance by 67 percent within eight months. Had they set the goal at a 10 percent increase they would have had a better chance of reaching their goal, but they preferred to reach, strain, and require creativity of themselves. They failed to reach their objective of 67 percent, but did reach their higher objective of stakehood by attaining a 60 percent increase—far ahead of where they would have been had they been willing to settle for "a little better than before." Nevertheless, the concept selected, whether (1) or (2), would depend upon the specific situation involved.

Stakes, wards, quorums, or individuals can set their own goals, but no one can set a goal for someone else. If the stake sets a goal for a ward or if a ward sets a goal for an individual, that becomes a quota. Quotas are not acceptable in Church administration. This means that the final responsibility for setting goals is that of the individual.

When Alma had taught his son Corianton about the plan of salvation, he concluded, "Therefore, O my son, whosoever will come may come and partake of the waters of life freely; and whosoever will not come the same is not compelled to come." (Alma 42:27.) Nevertheless, we are charged to "teach [our] children to pray, and to walk uprightly before the Lord." (D&C 68:28.)

"No power or influence can or ought to be maintained by virtue of the priesthood, only by persuasion, by long-suffering, by gentleness and meekness, and by love unfeigned; by kindness, and pure knowledge . . . reproving betimes with sharpness, when moved upon by the Holy Ghost; and then showing forth afterwards an increase of love toward him whom thou hast reproved, lest he esteem thee to be his enemy; that he may know that thy faithfulness is stronger than the cords of death." (D&C 121:41–44.)

"The basic decisions needed for us to move forward, as a people," President Kimball said, "must be made by the individual members of the Church. The major strides that must be made by the Church will follow upon the major strides to be made by us as individuals." ("Let Us Move Forward and Upward," *Ensign*, April 1979, p. 82.)

Brigham Young made it clear that priesthood members have the responsibility of keeping the temple busy. "The Priesthood," he says, "is for that purpose." (*JD* 18:213.) There are three basic units involved in fulfilling this important assignment: the temple, the stake, and the ward. Within those units there are certain key roles—those of temple worker, temple administrator, president of the high priests quorum, bishop, high councilor assigned to temple activity, high priest group leader, other Melchizedek priesthood quorum leaders, home teacher, and the individual himself. Each can set a goal relative to his own performance that, when achieved, will make an important contribution to the objective. When each one reaches and strains, maximum results are obtained. "Wherefore, now let every man learn his duty, and to act in the office in which he is appointed, in all diligence." (D&C 107:99.)

In 1841 the Lord commanded the members of the Church to build a temple in Nauvoo, outlined for them the ordinances to be performed therein, and then said: "And it shall come to pass that if you build a house unto my name, and do not the things that I say, I will not perform the oath which I make unto you, neither fulfil the promises which ye expect at my hands." (D&C 124:47.) President Kimball said, "The day is coming and not too far ahead of us when all temples on this earth will be going night and day." (Genealogy Seminar Address, 4 August 1977.) This is how we will accomplish "the things" the Lord said we must do.

At the dedication of the temple in Washington, D.C., President Kimball said, "It is imperative that we have temples and that we use them to their capacity. That I think we must keep in mind. Not just build, but fill." We know that "the Lord giveth no commandments unto the children of men, save he shall prepare a way for them that they may accomplish the thing which he commandeth them." (1 Nephi 3:7.) Therefore, let each adult in the Church qualify for temple service, then establish a schedule to come to the temple regularly and "do it" and thus fulfill the divine charge.

SAN DIEGO CALIFORNIA TEMPLE

Let thy bowels . . . be full of charity towards all men, and to the household of faith, and let virtue garnish thy thoughts unceasingly; then shall thy confidence wax strong in the presence of God; and the doctrine of the priesthood shall distil upon thy soul as the dew from Heaven.

The Holy Ghost shall be thy constant companion, and thy scepter an unchanging scepter of righteousness and truth; and thy dominion shall be an everlasting dominion, and without compulsory means it shall flow unto thee forever and ever.

◆

D&C 121:45–46

45

Planning for the Future

There is an old saying, "If you don't know where you're going, any road will do." (Anonymous.)

"The great thing in this world is not so much where we stand, as in what direction we are moving." (Oliver Wendell Holmes.)

"It is not only what we do, but also what we do not do for which we are accountable." (Moliere.)

The Apostle Paul said, "This one thing I do, forgetting those things which are behind, and reaching forth unto those things which are before, I press toward the mark." (Philippians 3:13–14.)

In most areas of the world people take vacations each year. Plans are made in advance as to how we will best use our vacation time. We start early. Our thoughts turn from dreams to anticipation. As the departure time nears, excitement sets in. We soon learn that the joy and satisfaction we receive is proportionate to how well we plan ahead.

Planning is the process of stepping into the future to a specific time and place, then looking back in order to gain perspective and asking oneself the question, "How do I get from where I am to where I want to be?" The answer to that question is the plan!

Most of us are good at setting goals. For example, we want to go abroad. We look into the future. We set the time and we select the place. Unfortunately, some of us don't do well at planning how we are going to get there or what we are going to do when we arrive. When we set a goal and prepare our plans well, we ensure a successful holiday.

Our first step in designing our plan is to read the travel brochures furnished by the travel agency. Then we go to the library and read what we can find that describes the points of interest and the things we can do upon our arrival. In short, we prepare ourselves by obtaining direction from reliable sources and design our plan accordingly.

If it is important to plan for a successful holiday lasting three weeks, how much more important it is to plan our trip into our next life extending eons into the future. We must prepare ourselves by studying reliable sources on where we want to go and how we can take full advantage of what our selected destination has to offer. Unfortunately, there are many travel agencies that have insufficient information to give us proper direction. They inform us about the destination *salvation*, but know nothing about the destination *exaltation*. They advise us that all roads lead to heaven, but they know nothing about the path that leads to the celestial kingdom, where we can perpetuate the most precious blessings mortality has to offer—family relations. The charge for their service is modest for it requires little or no personal sacrifice. As in merchandising, we get about what we pay for.

The road to exaltation in the celestial kingdom, however, requires personal sacrifice. It requires study, for no man can be saved in ignorance. It requires searching for the path that leads to both immortality and eternal life. It requires obedience to the laws and ordinances of the gospel established by God through his holy prophets. It requires faith in the Lord Jesus Christ, for he is the light and the way. It requires repentance of sin to satisfy the demands of eternal justice. It requires baptism by immersion for the remission of sins by one who has proper authority. It requires receipt of the Holy Ghost, who will become our constant companion and will be a source of knowledge and spiritual strength to assist us in reaching our proposed destination. It requires the Melchizedek Priesthood, which enables us to receive the greater knowledge and power necessary for the benefits that await us. It requires the fulness of the Melchizedek Priesthood, which can only be received in the temple of the Lord. The price is obedience and sacrifice.

Some travel agencies refer you to a salvation that is immortality or resurrection or the reuniting of the spirit and the body at a specific time after mortal death. No sacrifice is required, for immortality comes by the grace of Jesus Christ through his atoning sacrifice. But exaltation must be earned by obedience to the laws and ordinances of the gospel, starting with the offering of a broken heart and a contrite spirit. Our travel agency has a packaged plan for this remarkable adventure. But it requires effort, study, and sacrifice.

We are taught by the Spirit in the temple of the Lord to better understand the way and the destination. Thus the temple becomes a stepping-stone to help us in our journey from where we are to where we want to be—in God's presence—where he will share with us all that he has. We "press toward the mark," we know the road we should take, the direction we are moving, and what we need to do to get there. We invite all to accept God's plan for a trip into eternity by coming "unto him and partak[ing] of his goodness; and he denieth none that come unto him, black and white, bond and free, male and female; and he remembereth the heathen; and all are alike unto God, both Jew and Gentile." (2 Nephi 26:33.)

LAS VEGAS NEVADA TEMPLE

Great and marvelous are the works of the Lord,
and the mysteries of his kingdom . . . which
surpass all understanding in glory, and in
might, and in dominion . . . they are only to
be seen and understood by the power of the
Holy Spirit, which God bestows upon those
who love him, and purify themselves before
him; to whom he grants this privilege of seeing and knowing for themselves.

D&C 74:114, 116, 117

46

Preparing to Enter the Presence of the Lord

♦

A young man told me he had been called to be elders quorum president in his ward. The stake high councilor to whom he reported explained to him that he was to be responsible for the members of his quorum and their families. When a family whose head was an elder moved into the ward, he assigned a quorum member and his wife to furnish a meal the first evening of their arrival. After several successful assignments had been fulfilled, the wife of the next couple assigned said, "This is not the responsibility of the elders quorum, it is the responsibility of the Relief Society." The objecting wife spoke to her Relief Society president, the Relief Society president spoke to her bishop, the bishop called the elders quorum president to his office and said, "This is not the responsibility of the elders quorum, but the responsibility of the Relief Society."

The elders quorum president explained the instructions he had received from the stake high councilor to whom he reported and respectfully inquired, "Bishop, is the Relief Society auxiliary to the priesthood or is the priesthood auxiliary to the Relief Society?" The bishop seemed uncertain as to how to answer the question and left the matter for further consideration. My friend inquired what my answer would be. We discussed the coordinating role of the ward council and how the Relief Society and the priesthood should be coordinated so that the two could be yoked together in an effective relationship.

My friend told me he had invited the son of one of his elders to a basketball game. I counseled him first to coordinate such an invitation with the father in order to avoid conflict. Then I explained the following principle to him: When our Heavenly Father placed Adam and Eve on earth he did so with the purpose of teaching them how to regain his presence. They were taught the plan of salvation and were commanded by the Lord to be baptized and to receive the Holy Ghost. Then the Lord gave Adam the order of the Son of God. "To enter into the order of the Son of God is the equivalent today of entering into the fullness of the Melchizedek Priesthood, which is only received in the house of the Lord." (Ezra Taft Benson, "What I Hope You Will Teach Your Children About the Temple," *Ensign*, August 1985, p. 8.)

In the valley of Adam-ondi-Ahman Adam gave his righteous descendants his last blessing. Joseph Smith said that Adam blessed his posterity because "he wanted to bring them into the presence of God." (*Teachings of the Prophet Joseph Smith*, p. 159.) "How did Adam bring his descendants into the presence of the Lord? The answer: Adam and his descendants entered into the priesthood order of God. Today we would say they went to the House of the Lord and received their blessings. . . . Enoch followed this pattern and brought the Saints of his day into the presence of God." (Ezra Taft Benson, "What I Hope You Will Teach Your Children About the Temple," *Ensign*, August 1985, p. 9.)

> Now this [i.e., those principles spoken of in D&C 84:19–22 concerning the Melchizedek Priesthood] Moses plainly taught to the children of Israel in the wilderness, and sought diligently to sanctify his people that they might behold the face of God; but they hardened their hearts and could not endure his presence [today we might say they failed to qualify for a temple recommend]; therefore, the Lord in his wrath . . . swore that they should not enter into his rest while in the wilderness, which rest is the fullness of his glory. Therefore, he took Moses out of their midst, and the Holy Priesthood also. (D&C 84:23–25.)

Having reviewed this with my friend, I continued, "You said you were taking the son of one of your quorum members to the ball game. Tell me, Ric, what are you trying to accomplish in doing so?"

"I want to show him a good time," he responded.

"Now, Ric, you're an elders quorum president; you have a specific responsibility. You're striving to fulfill that responsibility. What is it you're trying to do?"

"I'm trying to make a friend of him."

"Now, Ric, you have a good mind; I want you to think through what we've just discussed and then answer my question. What is it you are really trying to do?"

He got the point and said, ''I'm helping to prepare him to enter the presence of the Lord.''

Whether we are an elders quorum president, a home teacher, a Sunday School teacher, a Relief Society president, a bishop, a Primary teacher—whatever our assignment is—we should be preparing all individuals under our charge to enter the presence of the Lord. When we understand this principle our efforts have a long-range focus. They all work to the end of preparing the individual for exaltation through the blessings of the temple. The emphasis of teaching the gospel, perfecting the Saints, and saving the dead should all be carried out with this objective in mind. When all of us understand and accept this concept there is no conflict, for we all strive for the same objective—to prepare the individual for eternal life with God in the celestial kingdom.

The temple of the Lord is a stepping-stone between mortality and eternal life. It prepares us through performance and compliance to enter the presence of the Lord and to enjoy eternal life with God the Father in the eternities to come. Therefore, let us come to the temple of the Lord regularly to prepare ourselves to enter his presence.

Temple de Toronto
Église de Jésus-Christ des Saints des Derniers Jours

Toronto Temple
The Church of Jesus Christ of Latter-day Saints

TORONTO ONTARIO TEMPLE

Therefore, verily I say unto you, that your anointings, and your washings, and your baptisms for the dead, and your solemn assemblies, and your memorials for your sacrifices by the sons of Levi, and for your oracles in your most holy places wherein you receive conversations, and your statutes and judgments, for the beginning of the revelations and foundation of Zion, and for the glory, honor and endowment of all her municipals, are ordained (set in order) by the ordinances of my holy house which my people are always commanded to build unto my holy name.

◆

D&C 124:39

47

The Ending That Is
Only the Beginning

◆

The Church of Jesus Christ of Latter-day Saints as the Lord's church, carries forward his objective, which is "to bring to pass the immortality and eternal life of man." (Moses 1:39.) The gospel of Jesus Christ is God's plan of salvation, designed to teach mankind how that objective can be obtained.

Immortality is a gift from the Savior that comes by grace alone and will be given to every man who is ever born. Those who receive eternal life will first receive immortality, which is to live forever in the resurrected state with body and spirit inseparably connected. Those who are worthy—that is, those who in mortality accepted the gospel of Jesus Christ, were baptized by proper authority, and conformed their lives to gospel principles; and those who died without knowledge of the gospel in mortality but were taught and accepted the gospel in the spirit world, and had vicarious baptism performed in their behalf—will be resurrected at the second coming of the Savior. The following thousand years, known as the Millennium, will be a time for organizing the family of Adam through genealogical research and by performing vicarious ordinances in the temple of the Lord for those who come under the clemency of Christ's atoning sacrifice. Those in the spirit world who are not resurrected at his second coming will be resurrected during the Millennium and at the end of the Millennium will receive their reward according to their works.

Following the Millennium those who are worthy of celestial glory will live on this celestialized earth in the celestial kingdom. "In the celestial glory there are three heavens or degrees; and in order to obtain the highest, a man must enter into this order of the priesthood (meaning the new and everlasting covenant of marriage); and if he does not, he cannot obtain it. He may enter into the other, but that is the end of his kingdom; he cannot have an increase." (D&C 131:1-4.)

"God's life is eternal life; eternal life is God's life—the expressions are synonymous. . . . Immortality is to live forever in the resurrected state. . . . Only those who obey the fulness of the gospel law will inherit eternal life. (D&C 29:43-44.) It is 'the greatest of all the gifts of God' (D&C 14:7), for it is the kind, status, type, and quality of life that God himself enjoys. Thus those who gain eternal life receive exaltation; they are sons of God, joint-heirs with Christ, members of the Church of the Firstborn; they overcome all things, have all power, and receive the fulness of the Father. They are Gods." (Bruce R. McConkie, *Mormon Doctrine*, p. 237.)

In premortal life before the world was organized:

> there stood one among [those that were spirits] that was like unto God, and he said unto those that were with him: We will go down, for there is space there, and we will take of these materials, and we will make an earth whereon these may dwell; and we will prove them herewith, to see if they will do all things whatsoever the Lord their God shall command them; and they who keep their first estate shall be added upon; and they who keep not their first estate shall not have glory in the same kingdom with those who keep their first estate; and they who keep their second estate shall have glory added upon their heads forever and ever. (Abraham 3:24-26.)

We kept our first estate, which was our premortal life. We are now in our second estate. One of the requirements to have celestial glory added upon us is to prepare ourselves through righteous living to enter into the presence of the Lord. To enter the presence of the Lord we must first receive the fulness of the Melchizedek Priesthood, which can only be received in the house of the Lord. (See Ezra Taft Benson, "What I Hope You Will Teach Your Children About the Temple," *Ensign*, August 1985, p. 8.) In this the dispensation of the fulness of times we are not confined to just one visit to the temple. We are encouraged to return regularly and represent by proxy one who is deceased. This gives us opportunity to renew the covenants we previously made with the Lord in the temple and to refresh our minds regarding the sacred ordinances we have previously received. Equally important is the role we fulfill as saviors on Mount Zion, wherein we open the door of celestial glory to those in the spirit world awaiting these supernal blessings. This opportunity enables us to further prepare ourselves to enter the presence of the Lord.

The criteria for doing so are (1) to develop faith in the Lord Jesus Christ, that he is the Only Begotten Son of God the Father, our Savior and our Redeemer; (2) to repent of our sins; (3) to be baptized by one having authority; (4) to receive the Holy Ghost under the hands of those holding the Melchizedek Priesthood; (5) to live in accordance with gospel principles; (6) to study the scriptures to learn and to keep our minds spiritually uplifted; (7) to strive to improve; (8) to receive one's temple blessings; and (9) to endure to the end. There is no other way. There is no shortcut.

If we had to prepare ouselves to enter the presence of the Lord without help from others it would be most difficult. To assist one another, we place our time, talents, and abilities in the hands of our priesthood leaders. They draw from that pool of talent to satisfy the needs of the individual members. By this process the Relief Society, Sunday School, Primary, and Young Men and Young Women organizations are staffed with officers and teachers to help the individual prepare himself. These organizations are adjuncts to the home in strengthening parents and in assisting them to teach their children to pray and walk uprightly before the Lord. It is important that the parents and each of those involved in this support system understand that the overriding objective, to prepare the individual to enter the presence of the Lord, be paramount. When we do so we become a team with a common objective.

As we prepare our own selves to enter the presence of the Lord and to do our part in building the kingdom of God, let us not strive only to see God through understandings, but also to behold him face to face as many righteous men in all dispensations of time have done. "And now, after the many testimonies which have been given of him," Joseph Smith said, "this is the testimony, last of all, which we give of him: That he lives! For we saw him, even on the right hand of God; and we heard the voice bearing record that he is the Only Begotten of the Father—that by him, and through him, and of him, the worlds are and were created, and the inhabitants thereof are begotten sons and daughters unto God." (D&C 76:22–24.)

To this I add my personal testimony that he lives; he is our Redeemer and our Savior; he is aware of each of us; he cares and is concerned; he is grieved when we sin and rejoices when we do right; he has gone to prepare a place for us; he will come again and help us prepare to go to the Father, to dwell in celestial glory where lie opportunities beyond our fondest dreams. Every ending is but a beginning. The ending of mortality is but a beginning that leads to immortality and eternal lives, to which I humbly and sincerely bear witness in the name of Jesus Christ, amen.

Index

◆